The Eco Guide to Sussex

Edited by Katie Ramsay

Introduction by Sarah Lew

Pegasaurus Publishing

www.pegasaurusbooks.co.uk/publishing

First Published by Pegasaurus Publishing 2010

© 2010 Katie Ramsay
© 2010 Pegasaurus Publishing

publishing@pegasaurusbooks.co.uk
www.pegasaurusbooks.co.uk/publishing

Printed and bound on FSC certified paper in the UK by imprintdigital.net: www.imprintdigital.net

ISBN 978-0-9566357-0-9

Cover design Katie Ramsay - Pegasaurus Publishing.
Cover illustrations by Richard Ellis www.RichardEllisFilms.co.uk and Lucy Irving www.irvingillustration.com.

Contents

ACKNOWLEDGMENTS.

This book is the product of months of tentative uncertainty and work. It is the first book produced under the Pegasaurus Publishing imprint and I am so proud and happy to finally be writing these words!

I decided to set up Pegasaurus Publishing late in 2009. I was fed up after graduating into a recession and after spending eight months travelling I felt inspired to do something creative and different. I have always loved writing and reading but I am fully aware how difficult it can be to succeed in such a competitive industry. Part of the ethos of Pegasaurus Publishing is to offer local budding writers and illustrators the opportunity to succeed and to encourage and showcase local talent from Sussex in Pegasaurus publications. All future books from Pegasaurus Publishing will follow this ethos. Sussex is a diverse county full of undiscovered talent. I want to discover this talent and work as a platform for writers, poets and illustrators to help them realise their dreams.

The eco guide to Sussex is not only promoting a fantastic cause but it is also showcasing some stunning illustrations from Sussex based artists and features articles from many budding writers.

This publication would not have been possible without the following people. Firstly the contributors! There is no way I could have written this book myself, I do not have the knowledge for a start. Without them this book would not have been possible. The enthusiasm that I received when I first approached possible contributors for the book was incredible. Everyone was so passionate and interested in protecting the environment and so dedicated to practicing this ethos in Sussex. A list of contributors is available at the end of each chapter and a full list is available at the end of the book.

Further thanks must go to my illustrators. I was overwhelmed by the quality of all the illustrations that I received and I am so happy to include their work. Illustrator information is also included at the back of the book.

I reached a point with this project where I was so close to the finish yet so far. I had all the text and all the illustrations and now I just had to put it all together. I could not have done this without the following people: Lucie Britsch, Nicky Carter, Danica Lesser, Sandra Pegram, Don Ramsay, Annika Thornton, Beth Williams and Ellie Wilson. My proof readers who gave their time to help me. Thanks also to Chris Nesbitt Smith for your consistent patience and advice.

I want to thank Alex Pegram for encouraging me to do this, for challenging me and most importantly for having faith in me. My family, especially my Mum Nicky and my sister Lucy for their continuous, never ending support and love. I want to thank my friends (they know who they are) for letting me bounce ideas off them so much and for generally just being there for me over the past few months and thanks to Rose Allett for all your incredibly helpful advice.

I want to thank Pegasaurus Books, www.pegasaurusbooks.co.uk

The title for this book was suggested by Ellie Wilson - thank you!

A massive thank you and dedication has to go to Natalie Skinner. Natalie provided me with the initial idea for this eco book over a couple of glasses of wine in the Open House back in November 2009. Without Nat this book would not have been born!

Last but not least, I want to thank Catherine Maris for helping arrange the book launch. Cat is planning to go into event organisation and I think it is a role she will be very good at!

Finally, I want to say thank you to anyone I have forgotten to mention who has helped me out along the way, there are so many people who have offered me advice it is difficult to mention them all!

I hope that everyone who reads this book will enjoy it and get something out of it. I want readers to realise that climate change affects us all. That, rather than relying on worldwide environmental summits and initiatives; that we can make small changes to our lifestyles and help to combat climate change on a local level.

Thank you.
Katie Jane Ramsay, July 2010

Katie Jane Ramsay is a twenty five year old Brightonian. Until the release of The Eco Guide to Sussex her biggest achievement to date was a trans-africa road trip completed with her boyfriend in 2009, before that it was completing a sociology degree from Birmingham University. Katie runs Pegasaurus Publishing alone, she is effectively a one woman band, and could not have finished this book without the help of numerous volunteers.

INTRODUCTION

By Sarah Lewis-Hammond

There are those who refuse to believe climate change is a real thing. We have a word for them, but it normally doesn't make it to print. Instead, here's what Professor Brian Cox, has to say on the matter: 'scientists reached a conclusion decades ago'.

Now that's settled, coming next in the great hierarchy of environmental action are people like me, and most probably you, who know something needs to be done but just can't figure out what.

It is a curious place in human history that we find ourselves. Behind is the greatest time of prosperity and abundance ever seen. Stretching out ahead is a heavy 100 years of uncertainty and insecurity. We sit here, wedged in the middle, not wanting to go back, unsure how to progress forwards.

We are at the forefront of technological achievement. We are able to send people into space and probes to the edges of our solar system, able to drill deep into the Earth, bringing back the remains of life from billions of years in the past, turning it into cheap and plentiful energy. We have eradicated illnesses that only fifty years ago killed our children with startling ease, and food has never been grown more in bulk than now.

1

But our technological advances have run away with us and it is all too easy to argue that socially we are struggling to keep up.

Our world is one where it is both acceptable and commonplace to fly food half way around the planet only to throw it in the bin, while back at the farm the growers themselves starve. It is a world where it is the done thing - the fashionable thing - to wear clothes we know are the product of violence and abuse. It is a world where success is measured in size, expense and attention rather than contentment, charity and virtue.

It is, then, no surprise that we feel immobile. Our society tells us the greatest winnings are to be found in constantly striving for more, our deepest instincts tell us on this path lies danger.

On a global scale, the systems available to us - politics, economics, our own evolutionary advantages - seem to be failing. Locally, it feels futile to change a light bulb and put out the recycling, and arrogant to then wash our hands and say we've done our bit. But in between the stasis of what we do and what we feel, in the middle of them and us, there is a space filled with action which is exciting, vibrant and growing.

It is a space where communities are coming together to build their own wind farms, or inventors are developing low impact building materials, or innovators are making energy out of fast growing algae. It is a space burning white hot with ideas. Of course, eighty per cent may well be mad, but twenty per cent might just work. And that's all we need.

Author Paul Hawken calls it the largest social movement in history, evolving organically with no name, figurehead or headquarters. He says: 'Like nature itself, it is organizing from the bottom up, in every city, town, and culture, and is emerging to be an extraordinary and creative expression of people's needs worldwide.'[1]

In both East and West Sussex we are amply represented. From the highly visible Brighton and Hove Food Partnership and their Harvest project, pushing for the city to be the urban food growing capital of the country, to the more hidden research departments at the universities of Sussex, Brighton and Chichester working on both technology and policy. There is a company in Haywards Heath claiming to have developed an internal combustion engine which will halve fuel consumption and in Lewes there is a magazine dedicated to discussions on green parenting.

And, of course, there is this book. Made for the you-and-mes of the world, who want to do something but just can't figure out what, who believe that the only way forward is together but have somehow become separated from the others.

Inside you will find a collection of essays, articles and information from people who were once you-and-mes but found a way to break out of the crippling stasis so many of us find ourselves in. They will guide you through the issues, help you take the first steps and introduce you to the community, to that togetherness that can seem so distant.

---

1   Paul Hawken, Blessed Unrest 2007 Viking Press New York

Lord Nicholas Stern, one time advisor to the government on the economics of climate change, says that we can't be certain of anything except that the risk facing us is enormous. Over the last five years, from a standing start, progress across the world has been extraordinary, and over the next five it will be more extraordinary still.

We have a tremendous opportunity to collectively use our unique ability to rationalise, to discuss and debate, to be both realistic and optimistic, and to work together to push through the thick fog of inaction to create a safer, cleaner, more stable world. This book is just the first step.

With thanks to Sarah Lewis-Hammond

Sarah Lewis-Hammond is an award-winning environmental journalist. Her weekly column in The Argus has been exploring sustainability in Sussex since 2006 and she has written for The Ecologist, The Guardian and The New Statesman. Sarah was the founding editor of ethical lifestyle magazine Rocks and created the Sussex Eco Awards.

The Sussex Eco Awards is an annual event celebrating environmental excellence displayed by people, projects or businesses in Sussex. The awards demonstrate that you do not have to be a dyed-in-the-wool hairshirt environmentalist to make a different but that the likes of you and me are out there in Sussex taking some action against climate change. www.sussexecoawards.org.uk

SECTION 1) CLIMATE CHANGE

Unless you have been living as a recluse for the past few years you cannot have escaped the media emphasis on the concept of climate change. But exactly what climate change is and how it is destined to affect us on a global and also individual level is something worth clarifying.

'Climate is the average weather experienced over a long period. This includes temperature, wind and rainfall patterns.'[1] The Earth's climate has changed throughout history. Just look back to the ice age to see how the climate has changed naturally since then. More recent examples of climate change however, have been attributed to us, the inhabitants of this planet and they seem to be happening not over hundreds and thousands of years, but now, in our lifetimes.

Global warming is a key component of the current debate surrounding climate change; put simply, carbonfootprint.com define global warming as 'the name given by scientists for the gradual increase in temperature of the Earth's surface that has worsened since the industrial revolution.'[2] It is this increase in temperature that will have negative effects on the environment that will ricochet across the globe.

There is a certain level of scepticism associated with the concept of climate change but the evidence is fairly incontrovertible.

1   Crown Copyright http://www.decc.gov.uk/en/content/cms/what_we_do/change_energy/what_is_cc/what_is_cc.aspx
2   Carbon footprint.com LTD: http://www.carbonfootprint.com/warming.html

In the past 100 years the average temperature on Earth has increased by 0.74 degrees Celsius and this rise looks set to continue.[1] Furthermore, looking at records that date back 159 years the ten hottest years have occurred in the last twelve years.[2]

There are three essential facets to this debate. It is useful to examine each in depth to obtain a good overall understanding of this debate: how does climate change affect the environment? What has caused it and how it can be prevented or the damage to our planet reduced?

How climate change affects the environment:

As I have already highlighted, the initial effect of climate change is an increase globally in temperature. Some people may celebrate the prospect of a warmer Britain, but in reality the effect of a global increase in temperature has far more disturbing consequences than simply being able to spend more time in the sunshine.

As the Department of Energy and Climate Change[3] along with Direct Gov[4] discuss there are a number of key changes that we are likely to experience globally. These include:

1   Crown Copyright http://www.decc.gov.uk/en/content/cms/what_we_do/change_energy/what_is_cc/what_is_cc.aspx

2   Crown Copyright http://actonco2.direct.gov.uk/actonco2/home/climate-change-the-facts/10-facts-you-should-know-climate-change.html#a2

3   Crown Copyright http://www.decc.gov.uk/en/content/cms/what_we_do/change_energy/what_is_cc/global_effects/global_effects.aspx

4   Crown Copyright http://www.direct.gov.uk/en/Environmentandgreenerliving/Thewiderenvironment/Climatechange/DG_072929

- rising sea levels: Oceans could completely submerge smaller islands and lead to coastal flooding elsewhere. Rising sea levels are a result of melting ice caps and glaciers due to increased temperatures. Direct Gov explain that sea levels could rise by between eighteen to fifty nine centimetres within this century.

- Flooding in poorer countries: It is argued that due to lack or resources and the ability to cope, developing countries will suffer more as a result of climate change.

- Food shortage and disease: It is anticipated that many regions will suffer food shortages as conditions will no longer be suitable for harvesting enough food in continents that rely on their crops such as Africa. In addition, diseases such as malaria could penetrate further afield.

- Water shortages: Rainfall will be more temperamental and we are all more likely to experience startling extremes of draught and floods.

- Loss of tropical forests: Direct Gov and DECC agree that our tropical rainforests will suffer as a consequence of unreliable rainy seasons and higher temperatures. We rely on rainforests to absorb CO2, if we lose this facility then even more CO2 will be released adding to the problems that the environment already has.

Information courtesy of DECC http://www.decc.gov.uk/en/content/cms/what_we_do/change_energy/what_is_cc/global_effects/global_effects.aspx Crown Copyright 2010
Direct Gov http://www.direct.gov.uk/en/Environmentandgreenerliving/Thewiderenvironment/Climatechange/DG_072929 Crown Copyright 2010

How climate change will affect us in Sussex.

- In the UK we may see extreme weather patterns becoming the norm.[1] Just think back to autumn 2009 and the extreme flooding in Cumbria, not to mention the persistent ice and snow that we were all subjected to in 2009 and 2010. Many people argue that these weather conditions are due to global warming. Southern Water reminds us that in recent years we have even seen snow in April![2]

- It is widely documented that we should expect a decline in the amount of rain fall during the summer months, this is depressing news as Daniel Campbell discusses in section two. In the south east of England we already have access to a lesser amount of water per person than the rest of the Country.

- On average the sea levels along the coast of Britain are ten cms higher than they were at the turn of the 20th century. It is argued that by 2080 water levels in the English Channel will have risen by fifty four cms.[3] Sussex lies along the South East coast so what does that mean for us?

- In Sussex effects of the sea breaching coastal defences can already be seen at Pagham where there is serious coastal erosion and increased risk of flooding. It has also been observed that East Head at the tip of Chichester Harbour could also be lost due to heavy storms. (As 3).

- There is yet another side to the effects of climate change which is often overlooked. In section eight of this book, Dan Danahar examines biodiversity and explains how it is seriously

---

1   Crown Copyright http://www.direct.gov.uk/en/Environmentandgreenerliving/
           Thewiderenvironment/Climatechange/DG_072929
2   http://www.southernwater.co.uk/Environment/ClimateChange/Default.asp
3   Copyright: UKCIP http://www.ukcip.org.uk/images/stories/Pub_pdfs/se_sum.pdf

threatened by climate change. We often neglect the natural habitats that surround us and lose touch with the wildlife that has for so long been part of this planet.

What has caused climate change?

It is argued that global warming occurs, to a large extent as a result of human activity and action on this planet. It is evident that 'we have altered the chemical composition of the atmosphere through a build up of greenhouse gases.'[1] However, just what are these notorious gases that cause climate change and how do we produce them? Greenhouse gases occur naturally and sustain and warm the atmosphere of the earth. However, in recent years and more specifically since industrialisation, increased levels of greenhouse gases have been released into the atmosphere. This is argued to lead to unnatural changes in the earth's atmosphere.

It is widely accepted that there are a number of gases that contribute to global warming.

- Carbon Dioxide (CO2) CO2 is deemed the greenhouse gas which is going to cause the most damage to the environment over the next 100 years.[2]

Others include:

- methane,
- nitrous oxide,
- sulphur hexafluoride,
- hydrofluorocarbons,
- perfluorocarbons.

1   http://www.carbonfootprint.com/warming.html
2   Crown Copyright http://www.decc.gov.uk/en/content/cms/what_we_do/change_energy/what_is_cc/grhouse_gases/grhouse_gases.aspx

Many organisations examine the relationship between human activity and an increase in the release of greenhouse gases. 'Act on Copenhagen' claim that since industrialisation in 1750 that there has been a thirty eight per cent rise in the level of CO_2 in the Earth's atmosphere. This amount of CO_2 that has been emitted has traditionally been attributed to the burning of fossil fuels such as oil, coal and gas as well as deforestation.[1]

It is widely agreed that in order to stall climate change we need to set about reducing our emissions of greenhouse gases. We produce green house gases in a number of ways: from driving our cars to heating our homes. Throughout this book we will look at how our daily lifestyles impact upon our production of greenhouse gases and how we are consequently affecting the environment.

You have probably heard of the concept of a carbon footprint. There are plenty of resources online that allow you to measure your carbon footprint and offer suggestions as to how you can reduce it. Before we discuss this it is important to understand what a carbon foot print is.

---

1   Crown Copyright http://www.actoncopenhagen.decc.gov.uk/en/ambition/achieve ments/december/copenhagen-pub-quiz/

What is a carbon footprint?[1]

Being able to measure our impact on the environment is critical in developing strategies to minimise it. It is easy to see the devastating effects of deforestation on ecology and habitats. But it is less easy to visualise what effects this destruction has on the atmospheric systems that govern global temperatures, and our ability to exist. As noted earlier it is accepted that the release of carbon (and other greenhouse gases) into the atmosphere is having an impact on global temperatures, and human activity is speeding up this process.

A carbon footprint is the amount of greenhouse gases produced in our day-to-day lives through burning fossil fuels for electricity, heating and transportation and so on. This footprint can be calculated for individuals and organisations alike, meaning that on all levels we can calculate, and act on, our environmental impact.

Our carbon footprint is measured in tonnes or kilograms. Although it is widely acknowledged that carbon dioxide is the most prominent green house gas, more commonly, a carbon footprint is taken to include all of the main greenhouse gases (mentioned earlier) that we produce as individuals and organisations. This can be measured as an equivalent to carbon dioxide production thus creating an overall record of our emissions. This is recorded as tonnes carbon dioxide equivalent (tCO2e). Combining calculations for the main green house gases and their global warming potential gives us a better idea as to what damage we are doing to our environment, how we are doing it and how we can reduce this impact.

---

1   What is a carbon footprint' written by Tom Chute and Katie Ramsay Information in this article is subject to: Copyright Carbon Footprint Ltd. www.carbonfootprint.com

During 2008 the total greenhouse emissions in the UK were estimated at 628.3 million tonnes carbon dioxide equivalent (tCO2e). Of this an approximately 532.8 million tonnes of carbon dioxide was produced.[1] There are a number of different suggestions available on the web as to what the estimated average carbon footprint for an individual in the UK is. Most estimates suggest it is between nine and ten tonnes of CO2 per year.

Essentially our carbon footprint is made up of a number of different things and can be split into two parts, the primary footprint and the secondary footprint.

1. The primary footprint is a measure of our direct emissions of CO2 or equivalent from the burning of fossil fuels including domestic energy consumption and transportation (for example: private and public transport, air travel and heating or lighting our homes). We have direct control over these emissions.

1   Crown Copyright http://www.decc.gov.uk/en/content/cms/statistics/climate_change/gg_emissions/uk_emissions/2008_final/2008_final.aspx

2. The secondary footprint is an measure of our indirect emissions. It includes buying things such as food, drink, toys and clothes. For example, imagine purchasing a banana that was grown in Uganda. Consider the level of emissions that are produced in the process of packaging and transporting that product from Uganda to a supermarket in the UK and then to your kitchen cupboard? This is quantifiable as your secondary carbon footprint.

Calculating ones secondary footprint precisely can be a very complex process, although companies and organisations are waking up to the idea that people care about the products they buy and their subsequent impact on the environment. It is becoming easier to make environmentally friendly choices due to improved labelling on the products we buy. This is especially true in the food industry, where it is possible to see the embedded emissions - CO_2e used to produce the item - labelled on some products.

Next time you pick up a product in the supermarket look to see if it has a carbon footprint figure. However, labelled or not, a general rule of thumb when thinking about environmentally friendly food shopping is buy local and buy produce in season which in general means that less heating, lighting and transportation has been involved in its production.

'What is climate change?' written by Katie Ramsay and 'What is a carbon footprint?' written by Katie Ramsay and Tom Chute sourced from carbonfootprint.com.

With thanks to www.carbonfootprint.com for information regarding 'What is a carbon footprint'. Copyright Carbon Footprint Ltd.

Carbon Footprint Ltd helps businesses & other organisations to reduce carbon emissions and energy use, comply with legislation and enhance their environmental brand image.

Section 2) Inside

We all waste energy at home and in the work place. Despite many of us having good intentions it's inevitable that we will waste energy somewhere. These individuals and organisations based in Sussex show us how we can save energy inside buildings - whether it is in our homes or in the workplace - and demonstrate how we can save some money at the same time!

Nigel's Eco Store, Green your home by Alice Doyle.

Nigel's Eco Store was set up in 2005. Driven by passionate people who want to make a difference, it has now grown into an inspirational online emporium of eco friendly products and ideas that solve environmental challenges.

Our core philosophy is to provide practical, functional, eco friendly, natural and organic products that are bought at reasonable prices. Our products are fun and desirable and compared to non-eco alternatives, do the same job, and look and feel just as great, or even better. When choosing products for our store, we ensure that they will save energy, that they are recycled and recyclable, biodegradable, made from sustainable sources and embody a low carbon footprint.

It is important that we help make eco choices easier for our customers. Shopping sustainably is an increasingly popular choice, and we realise that some work is needed to ensure that you are not giving to the environment with one hand, only to take away with the other. In selecting our products, we aim to inspire and motivate behavioural change by engaging with our customers on good buying decisions. We also provide our customers with the right information that they need in order to make their lives more sustainable, by way of newsletters and ebooks downloadable from our website.

Why eco?

Choosing to live more sustainably is becoming an aspirational lifestyle choice. Ecological issues and sustainability have moved from being a niche interest to becoming central on the mainstream agenda. There is an increasing move to localism and shopping online. The size of households is becoming smaller. Standards of comfort such as central heating are rising and affluence has led to the growth of home electrical appliances in number and variety. However, in parallel there has been a rise in energy bills, the recent credit crunch and climate change on the international agenda. In response to these events, ethical and ecological purchasing is on the increase as people seek to make their lives more sustainable and it is here that we are most able to assist.

How we help householders.

The word eco comes from the ancient Greek word 'oikos' meaning house, or the Latin 'oeco' meaning household. Our aim is to help our customers reduce their carbon footprint, cut energy bills and help everyone live a more sustainable life. In an era when governments have energy saving high on their agendas, and with energy costs soaring, being energy efficient in your home is one of the easier ways in which you can save money. And by saving energy, you'll be helping to fight climate change too.

Things to try.

A good place to start when trying to become more energy aware is to install an energy saving meter such as the Wattson. This will enable you to monitor and calculate the cost of running your home. If you find the number of household appliances increases, you can use standby energy saving kits to completely cut power to your household appliances at the flick of a switch. Hopefully householders will also consider making the change to a renewable energy supplier (where electricity is sourced from natural energy such as wind, the sun or running water). The average household that switches saves two tonnes of carbon dioxide (CO2) a year; this is the equivalent amount of emissions produced on a 5,000 mile journey in a petrol fuelled car.

Just changing the way we think about day-to-day tasks can help too. Try these simple energy saving tips for the home, which should help you to save money and reduce your carbon footprint.

Nigel's top ten energy saving tips for the home.

Switch off.
Did you know that an average family can save 150kg of CO2 a year just by turning things off? Appliances in standby mode

account for around ten percent of UK household energy use, so unplug devices when not in use, or invest in a standby saver such as the energenie standby shutdown. It's clever enough to recognise when you have put an appliance on standby, it will then automatically switch off the mains power to the appliance. Great for televisions, digital boxes and so on, and you can use it with more than one appliance as long as the max load of thirteen amps is not exceeded. An ecobutton can reduce your computer's carbon footprint by saving over 130kg of $CO2$ per year and save you up to fifty pounds. Every time you receive or make a phone call, go for a meeting or go for a break, simply press the ecobutton and your computer and monitor are put into the most economical sleep mode available.

Energy efficient lighting.

It is widely acknowledged that in most homes, lighting accounts for ten to fifteen percent of the electricity bill. Use a smart meter to compare the power consumption of normal light bulbs with that of low energy or energy saving light bulbs; you'll be amazed at the difference. Energy efficient lighting is eighty per cent more efficient than old fashioned tungsten bulbs.[1] They are reported to last up to ten times longer, saving you an estimated thirty seven pounds per year if you use them throughout your home.[2]

Rechargeable Batteries.

In the UK it is estimated that we throw away over 650 million batteries each year,[3] polluting the soil and filling landfill sites. Rechargeable batteries save energy and the slightly higher cost of purchasing them is recovered with just a few recharges. Recharging costs are also minimal. If you must use disposable batteries

---

1   Crown Copyright: http://www.defra.gov.uk/environment/business/products/road maps/lightbulbs.htm
2   Crown Copyright: http://www.direct.gov.uk/en/Environmentandgreenerliving/Energyandwatersaving/Energyandwaterefficiencyinyourhome/DG_179919
3   Copyright go-green-pc: http://www.go-green-pc.co.uk/eco-tips.php

then look out for battery disposal units in many high street shops. Use these instead of throwing away old batteries.

Change how you wash.
Try not to wash clothes on a setting above forty degrees Celsius. A wash at sixty degrees Celsius uses thirty per cent more energy. This is because ninety per cent of the energy used by a washing machine is used in heating the water. At the same time why not try an eco friendly washing powder such as Simply Laundry, a UK laundry product tht has been awarded the EU ecolabel, or soapods soap nuts; a natural laundry soap that literally grows on trees. Do you really need to wash everything after it has been worn just the once? And when you do wash, make sure you put on a full load and not a half load and you can save a further estimated forty five kg of CO_2 per year!

Dry clothes naturally.
Household appliances that give off heat such as tumble dryers, use lots of electricity. Whenever you can, hang your clothes outside to dry. Turning off the tumble dryer is a 100 per cent energy saving solution. If you have to use your tumble dryer and you're looking to save money and energy; for an eco friendly alternative to fabric conditioners you might want to try dryerballs. Dryerballs are safe, non-toxic and environmentally friendly; they will reduce your drying time by twenty five per cent and save on electricity subsequently saving you money.

Tips for buying energy efficient appliances:

- do some background research.
- Check if a product has any energy efficient features, such as automatic standby, which will turn an appliance off after a certain period if it is not used. Another useful feature is screen blanking which means you can use a TV for digital radio without using excess energy. Ask your sales person who can advise. And who can work out the running costs for you.
- Try combining electronics, such as televisions with inbuilt DVDs. Fewer products leads to a reduction in the amount of energy used.
- Some appliances are left on all day every day. If you're replacing your fridge, freezer, washing machine, dishwasher or kettle, look for the energy efficiency recommended logo which rates products for energy efficiency from A (best) to G (worst). Always aim for an A-rated appliance or as near as possible; really efficient models are labelled A+ or even A++.

Buy energy efficient appliances.

Eco kettles are great for saving energy and money! In particular the innovative eco kettle has a unique double chamber that allows you to measure out exactly how much water you want to boil, saving electricity, water, money and time. It is better for the planet... and you still get to have a great cup of tea.

Another example of new stylish products is the handpresso dome pod, a portable, handheld espresso coffee maker. Ideal for camping trips, holidays, travelling or even in the office; this light, stylish and easy-to-use coffee-making gadget is sure to impresso. Just fill the pod with your choice of coffee, and add boiling water, (preferably from an eco kettle).

If you need to replace or buy new products then make sure they are energy efficient.

Make the most of your home.

A quick and simple way to make your home warmer, and reduce your heating bills by over one hundred pounds per year is to use heatkeeper radiator panels. These fit behind the radiators and work by reflecting the heat that would normally be lost behind your radiators back into the room. Using them will cut your carbon emissions and improve the efficiency of your central heating. Furthermore, our radiator boosters have been flying out the door. For a running cost of around thirty pence per year, a radiator booster could save an average household between seventy and 140 pounds per year. It uses a small fan to capture the heat that comes out the back of your radiator, circulating it more efficiently around your room. It will heat your room faster, save lost energy, and reduce your heating bills. It can reduce heating time and cost by as much as fifty per cent. It's adjustable in size and has a built in thermostat too.

Save energy from your fridge.
It's a messy job but try defrosting the fridge and freezer to maintain efficiency. Use a savaplug which can save up to twenty per cent of the fridge's energy by regulating its power use more efficiently. The award winning savaplug saves you money on fridge and freezer running costs whilst being better for the environment. When fitted, it helps your fridge or freezer run more economically by adjusting the electricity supply according to the motor's needs. This means that there is less surplus energy being produced.

Cut back on your shower time.
A family of four could save 180 pounds per year, 40,000 litres of water and over 600kg of CO_2 just by showering instead of taking a bath. Taking a shower is considered to be better for the environment, and for your pocket, than having a bath. Why not try a shower timer? As water conservation becomes ever more important, this great water saving device will train you to save water when having a shower.

Taking a five minute shower every day rather than a bath drastically decreases the amount of water you will use. The average bath uses eighty litres of water whilst a five minute shower only uses thirty litres of water.[1] (Remember a power shower may well use more water than a regular shower.) Or you could install a single spray water saving showerhead and save up to sixty per cent (or up to 160 pounds per year) in water and energy costs by cutting down on the water that the shower uses, and ultimately saving you money on your water and energy bills.

Lower your thermostat.
Put on a woolly jumper. An extra layer means you can turn the heating down. Lowering your thermostat by just one and a half degrees can save up to ten per cent on your heating bills and significantly reduce the quantity of greenhouse gases that your household produces. Also don't forget to regularly bleed your radiators to get rid of inefficient air bubbles.

Consider solar powered or wind up alternatives?
Why not use a solar powered or wind up household gadget. You can buy wind up torches, wind up radios, and solar mobile phone and mp3 chargers. A wind up eco media player means you can watch favourite movies or music videos, listen to mp3 music files or tune into the radio anytime, anywhere. With eco wind up systems you never need worry about running out of

power or disposing of environmentally unfriendly batteries. And for those on the go, the solar gorilla laptop charger will charge your laptop using solar power. Its solar panels produce a staggering ten watts in direct sunlight, which is enough to run almost any portable electronic device including a laptop, notebook, mobile phone, satellite navigation system, iPod, and more.

What next?

A large proportion of the UK's carbon emissions come from the energy that we use every day, either at home or when we travel. If we are going to stand any chance of reducing our carbon foot print, we need to change our habits. This is a hard thing to do but being green is about being smart, about saving money, about making life easier and about being more self sufficient.

It is not just in our homes that we need to be more energy aware. Our workplaces, where we spend a lot of our time, must also be more energy efficient if we are to have a real impact. Karen Gardham shows us how we can all be kinder to the environment whilst at work.

Corporate responsibility and organisational efficiency, why reducing your environmental impact is good for business. By Karen Gardham.

Many people are addressing the environmental impact of their everyday lives, from using less energy, to reducing their food waste, to using more sustainable forms of transport. However, this enthusiasm does not always translate into actions in the work place.

This book illustrates why it's important to tackle our environmental impact, so why is this ethos often overlooked in the workplace, and why is it important for businesses to address their environmental impact? Here are some startling facts about the environmental impact of organisations:

- In the UK, business produces almost half of our carbon dioxide emissions.[1]
- UK industry uses a total of 1.3 billion cubic metres of water every year, three times more than is actually needed.[2]

1   Copyright The Carbon Trust: http://www.carbontrust.co.uk/cut-carbon-reduce-costs/reasons/why-save-carbon/pages/why-save-carbon.aspx
2   Copyright:Environment Agency 2010: http://www.envirowise.gov.uk/uk/Press-Office/National-Archive/The-Underwater-Office-businesses-urged-to-stem-the-tide-of-wasted-water.html

- A PC monitor left on overnight wastes enough energy to laser print 800 pages.[1]
- A photocopier left on overnight uses enough energy to make 3500 photocopies.[2]
- If each of the UK's ten million office workers used one less staple each day, 120 tonnes of steel would be saved each year.[3]
- In 1980 before the introduction of the PC, world office paper consumption averaged seventy million tonnes a year; by 1997 it had more than doubled to almost 150 million tonnes.[4]

Benefits to change.

The bigger picture according to the former Prime Minister Gordon Brown, suggests that over 400,000 jobs could be created over eight years through the move to a low carbon economy.[5] But even on an individual organisation-scale there are many benefits to taking action to reduce an organisation's environmental impact. These include:

- Saving your business money by reducing waste of all kinds.

Being green minded can make a big difference to your bottom line. Saving resources is an efficient way to do business, and can save a significant amount of money. With rising energy costs, being resource-efficient is becoming more important and can be the quickest way to save money. UK small and medium businesses (SMEs) waste around 1 billion pounds worth of energy each year, and could save around 1,000 pounds per employee a

1   Copyright: Environment Agency 2010: http://www.envirowise.gov.uk/article.aspx?o=313173&c=239916&l=1&p=9&af=FFFFFFFFFFFFFFFFFFFFFFFFFFFFFFFFFFFF

2   Copyright The Carbon Trust: http://www.carbontrust.co.uk/cut-carbon-reduce-costs/products-services/technology-advice/posters/Pages/poster-fact-calculations.aspx

3   http://www.foe.co.uk/campaigns/biodiversity/news/50_waste_tips.html

4   UK Wastewatch

5   http://www.number10.gov.uk/Page18530

year through basic energy efficiency.[1] A local authority in Sussex ran a waste reduction campaign in two of its offices and found that better facilities for recycling and mechanisms for staff to use fewer resources meant it reduced its waste by forty per cent in these areas, saving large amounts on waste removal costs as well as reduced stationery costs.[2]

- Differentiate you from your competition and attract customers.

Many people are concerned about environmental issues, and would choose a product based on the company's attitude to corporate social responsibility. A Department for Environment, Food and Rural Affairs (DEFRA) survey showed half of respondents would try not to buy products from companies whose ethics they did not agree with and would pay more for environmentally friendly products.[3] An Ipsos MORI poll indicated three quarters of British people consider that a company's environmental reputation would affect their purchasing decisions.[4]

- Improve recruitment and retention.

In tough economic times, recruiting talented staff is crucial. With more people caring about their individual environmental impact, working for a company who has an ethical approach to the environment is going to be inviting, and will make you stand out from other recruiters.

1   Copyright Environment Agency 2010: http://www.netregs.gov.uk/
2   Further info from Karen Gardham: http://www.greenminded.co.uk/
3   Crown Copyright: http://www.defra.gov.uk/news/2009/090923a.htm
4   Copyright Ipos MORI 2003: http://www.ipsos-mori.com/researchpublications/researcharchive/poll.aspx?oItemId=849

- Prepare you for changing government regulation and be risk-prepared.

Large public and private organisations that have used more than 6,000 MWh of electricity in 2008 will have to purchase and surrender allowances each year to cover their CO2 emissions under the CRC Energy Efficiency Scheme.[1] If your organisation, including any parent company and its subsidiaries, spends more than 500,000 pounds a year in the UK on electricity, you are likely to be included in the scheme. There are other pieces of legislation around waste, packaging and pollution that need to be adhered to by all organisations.

- Help you win contracts and grants.

Public sector organisations and many grant-giving bodies will require an organisation to have an implemented environmental policy in place before they award contracts or provide funds. Is your organisation able to demonstrate that?

- Be a responsible organisation.

We are damaging our environment at levels not seen previously, and some of this damage will be long term. Organisations have a large impact on the environment and being more environmentally aware can have benefits for a local and international community.

---

1   Crown Copyright: http://www.decc.gov.uk/en/content/cms/what_we_do/lc_uk/crc/my_org/my_org.aspx

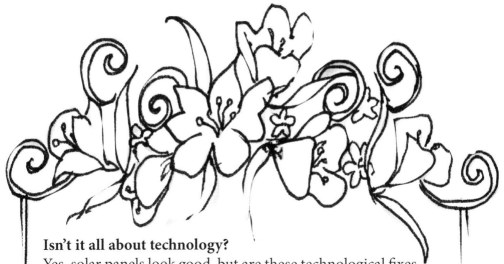

Isn't it all about technology?

Yes, solar panels look good, but are these technological fixes the answer to tackling issues such as climate change? Far from it. Whilst an organisation can install new technology, it needs to be used appropriately by staff. Consider this example. I buy a new hybrid car. It replaces my older diesel car. I feel great. I can drive with impunity now because I've done my bit for the environment by lowering my transport emissions. But have I? The car may have very low emissions, but it does still have some emissions. Whilst before I tried my hardest to cycle and walk more as I knew my old car was polluting, now my behaviour has changed and I'm using this car more because it's 'ok', so I may even be creating more emissions than before when I hardly used my car.

It is also a whole new product; think about all the pollution and resource use involved in making a new car. Furthermore, the roads I'm driving around on are not exactly impact-free in their making, from the materials used, to the habitats destroyed to create them. I may have made a good technological choice for the environment, but without the corresponding low impact behaviour it may not be worth very much.

Six steps to change.

Large or small, there are many things an organisation can do to reduce its negative environmental impact by following these six steps.

1. Find champions in your organisation.
    Don't start alone; find like-minded people in your workplace who can persuade the people in their teams that taking action is a positive and practical thing to do.

2. Build a case for change.
    Think about the business case for taking action, as outlined above. Take this to senior management, directors or trustees and demonstrate why taking action is good for business.

3. Assess where you are – base-lining.
    If you are not aware of your environmental performance at the moment, how will you know if you're improving, and by how much? An audit of your impact can be carried out in as much detail as you require. At a minimum, you should gather information from bills on how much energy and water you use, and check your waste transfer notes to see how much waste you send to landfill. The building manager for your organisation or for the company who runs the building you use should be able to help with this. Assess how much people travel for work by checking expenses claims for car mileage and train tickets.

4. Consult with stakeholders to develop your policy, based on your key areas of impact. Think about what issues are important to you as a business, how will this policy match your ethos, and that of your stakeholders? Use this as a basis to develop your environmental policy. Your policy should identify

your environmental impacts, identify a senior person who is responsible for the policy, set targets and resources needed to meet those targets, make a commitment to continual improvement and training for staff in understanding the policy, outline how the policy will be communicated both internally and externally, and be signed by the Chief Exec.

5. Develop an action plan with key staff who will lead on delivering targets in their area of work. The policy will need to be backed up by an action plan that will ensure you start making changes. Link each action to a member of staff whose responsibility it is to ensure that the action is carried out. These actions should be in their normal work plan. Once you have done your audit, you will know where your main areas of impact are, and therefore what targets to set, depending on how ambitious you are in improving your performance. You may want to look at all the work you have done so far and set up a formal environmental management system to monitor your performance.

6. Train all staff in their role in delivering the action plans and changing the culture of the organisation. You will need more than technological changes (see page 29). All staff need to read and understand the policy at a minimum, and ideally all be trained in why and how to reduce their environmental impact. Key staff delivering targets may need specialist training and support. However, many actions are simple and should be assigned to the person whose role is most aligned to it. For example, building managers will understand how to monitor energy and make the building more energy efficient, and will understand the business need to use resources most efficiently, it may just need to be made more of a focus of their role, with set performance targets around reducing energy use.

<u>Key ways to encourage behavioural change in the office:</u>

- Incentivise through competitions, special offers, rewards for behaviour change and innovative ideas

- Lead by example so people know how to change, and so they know that others are prepared to make the change

- Explain the reasons why you are making changes

- Make it as easy as possible, using technology, for example, set the printer up to automatically print double sided, or through simple means like putting a magazine file on desks where people can keep paper they've only used one side of for scrap paper.

- Give feedback when things are going well and where people have made a beneficial difference for the environment.

- Most importantly, consult on all changes: ensure staff feel involved in any changes that affect them by giving them input into the process.

But what can I do right now?

Keen to get going? Consider implementing some of these tips immediately or in the near future, whilst working to create a policy framework for delivering continual improvement. Many of these tips will also save an organisation money.

Energy.
- Turn appliances off when not using them, particularly lights, computers (monitors use half as much energy when left on with no computer as to when they are be ing used) and chargers, which keep using electricity after the appliance is unplugged if they remain switched on.
- Don't use energy if you don't have to, for example is the heating on in a room that isn't used very often?
- Insulate and draft proof your building
- Make the most of natural light
- Invest in energy efficient equipment, try to get a loan from the Carbon Trust.
- Maintain equipment and test it regularly so you know it is working efficiently.

Waste.
- You can't beat the waste hierarchy – reduce, reuse, recycle. Reduce; ask yourself whether you need that item in the first place. If you don't need it then don't get it. Then start to reduce the waste that you have been creating. For example, always print double sided to reduce paper use; if you do really need to print out emails press 'print preview' first to check you are not printing any unnecessary pages; change your margin widths on documents so you can fit more on each page that you print.

- Reuse; get more out of the item you're using. For example, refill printer ink cartridges, if you make a mistake printing on one side of a sheet of paper, use the other side to take notes or put a few sheets together to make a note-pad, reuse packaging boxes and filler, donate furniture not needed anymore to charity.
- Recycle; contact your local recycling company and recycle as much as possible including paper, cardboard, plastic bottles, cans, glass, textiles. Don't forget to close the loop; while you're busy recycling all that material it needs a market to go to. Buy recycled products.

Transport.
Transport accounts for twenty three per cent of domestic carbon emissions in the UK.[1] Reducing travel by unsustainable means is a key goal for many businesses.
- Before you travel anywhere, question whether it is a necessary trip, or whether this work could be conducted in any other way? Flying can have the biggest impact on your carbon footprint. Telephone or video conferences can be an efficient way to 'meet'.
- Use public transport wherever possible, develop a staff travel plan to promote and incentivise more sustainable forms of travel. For example, if you are a large organisation, you could try and negotiate low cost travel passes with the local bus company.
- Give a mileage allowance for staff that use their bicycles for work use.
- If members of staff are driving to work encourage them to car share.
- For any driving that has to be done, provide staff with fuel efficiency training.

1   Crown Copyright: http://actonco2.direct.gov.uk/actonco2/home/what-you-can-do/
        On-the-move.html

Water.

Only a small fraction of the earth's water can be used for drinking. Often forgotten, water is a precious resource that we need to protect, yet we are literally flushing fresh drinking water down the toilet.

- Fix a dripping tap as soon as possible
- If a cistern was made before 1993 it probably uses more water than it needs, so use a 'hippo' device (ask Southern Water for one) in the cistern, which can save up to three litres per flush
- When replacing urinals get waterless ones.
- If you have an outside landscaped area, ensure a water butt collects water for watering plants
- Invest in water efficient equipment – the Enhanced Capital Allowance (ECA) scheme enables businesses to write off 100 per cent of the cost of qualifying plant and machinery against taxable profits in the first year of purchase.[1]

---

1   http://www.eca.gov.uk/

Purchasing.

So, you've thought about the things your organisation does that directly affect the environment. But what about the things you are purchasing? Watch out for greenwash. Be wary of labels such as

'Natural', 'Green', 'Environmental', 'Sustainable'

They are not protected terms and they do not mean a thing unless you know how the product has been made, what it contains, and what impact its use will have.

Some labels to look out for to verify the environmental credentials of a product include:

- EU Ecolabel: this voluntary scheme allows the Eco label logo to be used for products and services that meet strict environmental criteria. http://www.eco-label.com
- Soil Association: certified organic – anyone processing a food product which they want to market as organic need certification, and one of the best known ones is provided by the Soil Association. http://www.soilassociation.org/
- Fairtrade Mark: in the UK the Fairtrade Mark ensures a product meets the standard of the international fair-trade certification body. As well as ensuring workers get a fair wage for their work, did you know that Fairtrade standards require producers to reduce synthetic pesticide use, reduce energy use and waste, protect biodiversity, and bans the use of GMOs? http://www.fairtrade.org.uk/
- FSC: Forest Stewardship Council runs a global forest certification scheme. This system allows consumers to identify, purchase and use timber and forest products produced from well-managed forests. http://www.fsc-uk.org/

When you're making purchases, ask questions such as:

- Do I actually need this product in the first place, or can I use another item for the same job, refurbish a current product?

- Does the company I am buying from have an environmental policy and an environmental management system?

- What materials is the product made from, are they renewable or recycled?

- How far does the product travel when it's being delivered to the workplace?

- How many chemicals are used in the product?

- How much energy does the product use during use?

- How long will it last?

- Is the product easily repairable if it breaks down?

- Is the product reusable or recyclable when I have finished using it?

Whole life cycle.

When buying something, think of the 'whole life cycle' of the product. If you were buying a washing machine based on the cost, you would take into account not only the purchase cost but the running cost of the machine over its whole life.

If Machine A cost 450 pounds, lasts ten years and costs twenty pounds a year to run, the total cost over five years would be 550 pounds. Machine B may only cost 350 pounds to purchase, but if it only lasts five years and costs forty pounds a year to run the total cost over five years would also be 550 pounds but you would have to buy a new machine, so the cost would be higher!

Do the same analysis on any items you're purchasing, and look at it in terms of its environmental impact. Don't just consider how much energy it uses to run it and how long it lasts, but consider the energy it took to make the machine, the pollution that may have been caused by its manufacture and extraction of materials for parts, whether parts are replaceable, is it reusable. The impact of an item can occur way before you've bought it and started using it. For example, one ounce of gold can produce up to thirty tons of toxic waste before it is even made into a ring...

What next?

Organisations in the UK, from the largest businesses to the smallest charities, have an enormous potential to improve their environmental performance. There is a robust business case for doing so, as well as a strong moral case to leave the planet in a better state than we found it, for us and for future generations and species.

There are a number of resources available online to help you If you want your workplace to be a more eco friendly place. Details are available at the end of the chapter.

We have already looked at some of the adverse effects of climate change that will affect us in the UK if we are not careful. Brighton and Hove resident Daniel Campbell has done some research into the potential water shortages that we could suffer in Sussex and offers some suggestions as to how we can deal with this.

Sussex water by Daniel Campbell.

The phrase 'global warming' is powerful. It conjures up a whole host of visceral images; polar ice caps cracking and melting, oceans rising, great droughts sweeping over entire countries, and various other catastrophes horrific and terrifying enough to make a Hollywood special effects department doff their caps. These are indeed some of the very frightening, very real dangers of climate change, but they're still rather distant to us here in Britain. Although typically the worst we have to contend with is an extra cold winter coupled with an occasional hosepipe ban, climate change is very much a present threat, affecting our lives in much more furtive, but no less worrying, ways.

I don't need to explain to you what climate change is; as a phrase, it more or less does what it says on the tin. What is less obvious, though, is the effect it's having on us, and specifically on our water supply.

Notably it's creating extreme weather such as droughts and storms, as well as affecting the amount of rainfall we receive, which has an impact on farming and irrigation. Climate change is also causing greater soil movement, making our drinking water supply pipes more prone to cracking. Sea surface temperatures are getting warmer, which, along with the melting polar ice caps, is causing sea levels to rise.

As a race, we have a good relationship with water. We like it a lot. It's probably the single most important resource we have (after all, we can survive for thirty or forty days without food, but only five days without water), and we are lucky to live in a country where it is fresh, clean, and available to everyone; all we need to do is turn on a tap.

However, despite our typically soggy climate, the reality is that we do not have as much water at our disposal as you may think. For instance, in England and Wales we have 1,334 cubic metres of rainfall for each person per year. This is far less than most European countries, as well as less than Ethiopia (1,519 cubic metres), Afghanistan (2,608 cubic metres) and less than half of the water per person for Iraq (2,917 cubic metres).[1]

Because of its high population and low rainfall, people in the south east of England experience less rainfall per person than the rest of the country, yet despite this, we still use water as if it were, well, water. In the UK, on average, each person uses 150 litres of water a day,[2] about the equivalent of forty five cans of coke.

---

1   Kingspan Water: http://www.kingspanwater.com/pdf/tech_brochure.pdf
2   Copyright Environment Agency 2010: http://www.environment-agency.gov.uk/homeandleisure/drought/38519.aspx

Shockingly, Southern Water suggests that only three per cent of our water is used for cooking and drinking.[1]

So then, what can we do to save water without constantly and meticulously monitoring our water consumption? After all, we are lucky enough to live in a place where we do have easy access to clean water, then the last thing we should do is squander it. Here are some simple, everyday tips to help you increase your water use efficiency, and reduce your water bills while you're at it.

- Put a save-a-flush bag in your toilet cistern. These bags (available free of charge from Southern Water's website) are filled with granules that soak up water and expand to raise the water level in the cistern, saving one litre of water each time you flush.

For a quick alternative, a large, heavy item, such as a large plastic bottle filled with water, will do the same kind of thing in a pinch, but be careful not to use an object that will break apart over time, like a concrete brick, as this could damage or break your toilet.

- Take showers, not baths. According to Southern Water, a bath uses around eighty litres of water whereas a shower averages at around thirty litres.[2] The chances are, unless you're in an extremely physical job, you aren't going to get that dirty, so by taking a brief, five minute shower you stand to save around fifty litres of water, and you'll still be squeaky clean. If you have been mud-wrestling today, however, then aim to spend under fifteen minutes in there, twenty minutes maximum.

- If the idea of a time limit in the shower doesn't appeal, you could always install an economic, water-reducing shower

---

1   http://www.southernwater.co.uk/pdf/education/ks3ADripInTime/dit_fact_sheets.pdf
2   Copyright Southern Water: http://www.southernwater.co.uk/homeAndLeisure/waterEfficiency/atHome/

head. A five minute shower with an ordinary shower head every day can use up to 45,000 litres of water a year, whereas a water-reducing shower head can cut that amount down to just 16,500 litres.

For a free way to push down your water usage in the shower, the excellent polluteless.com advises you to take a coin the size of a penny, drill a 1/16" hole in it, and place it between the shower head and the water line. Your shower, it says, at common household water pressure will now use less than one gallon of water per minute, even at full force.[1]

- Keep a reservoir of rain water. This is one of the simplest tips, but also one of the most useful and it's sustainable, too. You can buy large, modern, plastic water butts specifically for this, but all you really need is a decent sized container, like a bucket or even a trough, if you can get your hands on one. Then, simply put it outside and wait for the English weather to do its stuff.

Rain water can be used for a wide variety of things, like watering the garden, washing the car, filling up your toilet cistern, and even doing the laundry in. You could even install an internal rainwater tank and have a plumber connect it to your toilet cistern (although this may lead to regrets during summer time).

- Don't leave the taps running. This one sounds obvious, but just by leaving the tap running while brushing your teeth alone can waste up to six litres of water per minute. Also, fix your dripping taps. They might not seem that offensive, but a tap that drips once a second could waste up to 10,000 litres of water a year,[2]

---

1   Copyright Karsten Weiss Pollute less: http://www.polluteless.com/Advice_Water_ Consumption.html
2   Copyright Southern Water: http://www.southernwater.co.uk/homeAndLeisure/wa terEfficiency/atHome/tipsforyourhome.asp

and a tap left dripping for a single day could waste enough water to run a shower for five minutes.

One solution to this problem is to remove the connection from your sink to your drain and instead have a water butt underneath the basin. This is a far more sensible idea than it sounds because, as well as ensuring that no drips are going to waste, most of the water that flows down your sink's plughole is what we call 'grey water', water that has been used but isn't really dirty. This water can, like rain water, be used for all kinds of things that you'd normally use perfectly good drinking water for.

However, if that sounds like too much effort then Southern Water's website has a short, simple guide to fixing the most common instigator of tap-trouble, worn out washers.

- Be sensible. Think before you turn on your hosepipe. Do you really need it? Hoses can use up to 1000 litres of water an hour, and there isn't much you can do with a hose that you can't with a bucket of water (collected from your brand new homemade water butt, of course) and a little bit of effort.

Also, try to cut down on using your washing machine. Depending on the amount of people in your household, you could try assigning yourself a set number of laundry days a week, ensuring that your washing machine is as full as you can safely get it before turning it on.

You may want to invest in a water efficient washing machine; this can reduce the amount of water used by sixty five per cent.

While handy, dishwashers are big water consumers, using about thirty seven litres of water per load. Again, there are water efficient models available, but it's far more environmentally friendly, (and cheaper) to don the marigolds and wash your plates by hand.

These simple tips may not seem like much, but even following just one of them can make a huge difference: if just one in one hundred people in Brighton and Hove swapped a bath for a shower once per week, we'd save over three million litres of water in six months. If one in a hundred households in Brighton and Hove fixed their leaky taps, in six months we'd save over five and a half million litres.

The fact is, saving water isn't hard or expensive, and you don't need to chain yourself to anything to do it. It can be as simple as turning off a tap.

With thanks to: Daniel Campbell for the text regarding saving water and Void X for the statistics that he based on the 2001 census.

Daniel Campbell lives in Hove with four cats, two manic depressives and a girl. As well as journalistic articles he also writes fiction, and is available for weddings, barmitzvahs and children's birthday parties.

Void X wears his sunglasses at night.

Alice Doyle, Press and Marketing Manager at Nigel's Eco Store. Nigel's Eco Store - www.nigelsecostore.com sells a wide variety of energy-saving products. An online retailer of environmentally friendly products inspired by stylish, innovative and functional eco design, Nigel has handpicked a variety of products and gifts that'll help you to save money, reduce your carbon footprint and live a more planet-friendly life. The range features something for everyone including home furnishings, kitchenware, gadgets, office products, kids' toys and energy-saving devices.

All products sold by Nigel's Eco Store are environmentally sound. Made of organic, recycled and energy efficient materials, they will not only look great in your home, but will help to reduce your contribution to global warming.

Karen Gardham is a freelance sustainability consultant, working across London and the south east of England to help organisations be more Green Minded. Karen has over ten years experience of award-winning environmental campaigning, policy making, and action planning. Her work has helped organisations save money and resources, and embed efficient working practices into their operations. Her experience of working in the private, public and not-for-profit sectors has led to an understanding of the differing pressures they face and how to succeed within them.

She started Green Minded to help organisations of all sizes create a positive impact on the environment and society, creating a culture where corporate social responsibility is not only the norm, but a desirable way to run a business.
www.greenminded.co.uk

Further thanks to:

Karsten Weiss at Pollute Less, www.polluteless.com

Kingspan Water - part Kingspan Group PLC, a leading manufacturer of sustainable products for the construction industry. Kingspan Water is a range of rainwater harvesting and greywater recycling products and is part of the group's environmental division that also manufactures off-mains drainage, pumping, stormwater attenuation and fuel storage systems.

Southern Water – Southern Water supplies fresh, quality drinking water to more than one million households and treats and recycles wastewater from nearly two million households across Sussex, Kent, Hampshire and the Isle of Wight. http://www.southernwater.co.uk/

Further resources to help you make your workplace greener: WRAP
WRAP works in the UK to help businesses and individuals reduce waste, develop sustainable products and use resources in an efficient way. www.wrap.org.uk

The Carbon Trust
The Carbon Trust is a not-for-profit company providing specialist support to help business and the public sector cut carbon emissions, save energy and commercialise low carbon technologies. www.carbontrust.co.uk

Business Link
Lots of advice on reducing your environmental impact and setting up an environmental management system. Useful tools on identifying where you can save money by going green, and what

environmental legislation effects you.
www.businesslink.gov.uk/environment

Net Regs
Online information about environmental legislation
www.netregs.gov.uk

Enhanced Capital Allowances scheme
Enhanced Capital Allowances (ECAs) enable a business to claim 100 per cent first-year capital allowances on their spending on qualifying plant and machinery. There are three schemes for ECAs:
- Energy-saving plant and machinery
- Low carbon dioxide emission cars and natural gas and hydrogen refuelling infrastructure
- Water conservation plant and machinery
www.eca.gov.uk

Every Action Counts
Advice for community and voluntary sector organisations on sustainable development. Although the campaign is no longer active, the website still contains useful guides.
www.everyactioncounts.org.uk

Brighton & Hove Green Pages
A guide to greener living, featuring many local businesses in Brighton & Hove and around.
www.brightongreenpages.org

Book of Green
Featuring many green and ethical businesses across the UK, this guide is available online and in hard copy.
www.bookofgreen.co.uk

Section 3) Outside

You may not realise it but everyone can grow their own food, regardless of the amount of space they have. Whether it's growing crops in an allotment, a few potatoes in your garden or some salad leaves on your window pane. We hear from the experts in a bid to encourage all of us to experiment a bit more with growing our own food.

There are a number of organisations and initiatives in and around Sussex who can point us in the right direction, whether we want to become self sufficient or just supplement our grocery shopping.

Harvest Brighton and Hove is all about growing your own and eating local food. From window boxes to community allotments, there are opportunities for everyone to join in. Harvest has brought together lots of different organisations who are interested in food and who can help you learn how to grow your own, make use of surplus produce and eat more locally produced food.

Harvest aims to increase the amount of food grown in the city: on windowsills, in back gardens, in allotments and in community spaces like parks and around housing estates. They go scrumping apples from trees around the city to prevent waste and make delicious juices and chutneys. Harvest is also running a programme to distribute surplus allotment produce to community food projects like lunch clubs and cookery sessions. There are plenty of opportunities to get involved: through volunteering at a project, attending a training course or getting involved in a community food event.

If you want to learn how to grow some of your own food or you already do, or if you just want to eat more local food, then Harvest is for you!

Before offering you advice about how to grow your own food it is important to understand why we should. For a start we need to assess the health, environmental and economic benefits. Jess Crocker, Sarah Waters and Ann Baldridge from Harvest Brighton and Hove tell us more.

Why grow your own? By Harvest Brighton and Hove.

Ever thought about growing your own food or learning more about how food is grown? There are plenty of opportunities to get outside, get your hands dirty and give it a go. Growing your own food can be a very rewarding experience. There's nothing better than planting a seed, watching it grow and then eating the results. It is as fresh as can be, and healthy, so why not give it a try? Whether you have an allotment, garden or just a balcony or windowsill there is plenty you can do!

Five reasons to grow your own:
1. It is healthier in terms of diet, exercise and looking after the planet.
- Gardening is often referred to as the green gym! Gardening not only gets you physically fit but also benefits the mind, providing a connection with nature that is often sorely missing in our busy urban lives.
- Many crops lose their nutritional value as soon as they

49

are picked so getting your vegetables straight from the plot to the plate will help you get the most from your food.
- Also think about the difference in taste. Have you ever compared the flavour of a freshly picked sun-warmed tomato with a supermarket shelf variety? There is no comparison; a home-grown tomato wins on the taste test any day. Try it!

2. It is a good way to get cheaper, better food for you, your family and friends.
- Once you get into the swing of growing your own produce the money-saving potentials are huge. Even with a small balcony and a bit of effort you can provide your family with a variety of great tasting salad leaves for most of the year.

3. It is more sustainable (less waste, fewer food miles and less packaging).
- Growing your own produce can benefit the local environment too. Vegetables, fruit and flowers all provide food for a wide variety of insects. Your compost bin can make a great winter home for a range of insects, amphibians and mammals as well.
- Consider how far your food travels. Next time you are in the supermarket have a look at where your vegetables were grown. Do you need to buy those French beans flown in from Kenya? Think how many air miles and how much pollution could be saved if you grew them in your own garden.

4. You develop a closer relationship with the seasons.
- Eating home grown food means eating seasonal produce. Certain vegetables and fruit grow more easily at certain times of the year and eating with the seasons means that you're eating what nature intends you to eat. Eating seasonal, local food helps us appreciate our food; it reduces the burden on the environment (food

does not have to be flown in or grown in heated glasshouses); it is abundant and often less expensive; and it tastes great.

5. Greater self-reliance and a sense of satisfaction with what you've grown.

- We can all do our bit to help the environment by growing some of our own produce and it doesn't have to involve huge amounts of money, time or even effort.

I want to grow but I don't have anywhere to do it…

One option is to join the allotment waiting list. Harvest Brighton and Hove are working with the local council to bring back into use allotment plots that have not been used for up to sixty years, so the waiting list is shrinking. However, you might still have to wait and furthermore, many new growers can find a large allotment plot overwhelming or too time consuming.

So why not look again at what space you do have? You can grow a surprising amount on even a small patio, balcony or windowsill. Alternatively, why not look for other ways to access land? The local Grow Your Neighbour's Own scheme matches up garden-owners who aren't using their land with keen gardeners who are looking for space. Or you could find a plot yourself: why not find out who owns that vacant lot or green space in your neighbourhood and see if you can get growing there?

There are also lots of great community food projects around the city which you can get involved with. They all have regular volunteer work days where you can learn about growing and share the rewards. The Harvest website lists many of these projects which are located all around the city. They have also set up a vegetable patch where people can volunteer right in the middle of Preston Park!

I've got land! A quick guide to growing your own by Harvest Brighton and Hove and Tanya Sadourian.

Things to consider before you get started.

Sun, shade, wind, soil depth, slope and flatness of the land, drainage and security all need to be considered before planning your site. This will save you time, effort and prevent a lot of potential problems. Planning your plot will help you to see that once broken down into steps the site is manageable. It will also save you time and effort.

Equipment.

Think about what equipment you will need to grow your own food. For a container garden (containers aside) a trowel and a watering can with a rose will suffice. If you have a plot, add a spade, fork, hoe and rake. A good fork is an essential buy. If you are buying secateurs, get the best you can afford; they will last. A plank of wood is very useful for you to walk on without compacting the soil. Leather garden gloves will also be helpful. On a plot you may also need a shed or a place to store tools, a water source or water butt to collect rainwater, a compost bin, space for wildlife and a seating area where you can rest and appreciate all your hard work. Think about how to get around your plot (possibly with a wheelbarrow).

Be sure to check local networks like Gumtree, Friday Ad and Greencycle for cheap or free tools and materials.

If planting in containers, they should not be smaller than thirty centimetres, and ideally much larger. Avoid terracotta as it dries out quickly. Using a large container is best; hungry plants will have more chance to grow into the available compost. Go for a loam rather than multipurpose compost, as it holds more nutrients and retains water better.

Preparing your plot; getting rid of weeds.

Good crops need good growing conditions so that means starting with a weed-free patch. If your patch is very overgrown and you feel overwhelmed with the thought of clearing away the brambles, grass and numerous weeds, persevere; it will be worth the effort. Take it step-by-step and it will be cleared sooner than you think.

It can be discouraging to clear a space of land only to have the weeds return larger and stronger within weeks! If you aren't going to grow in the space immediately, mulch it. Mulching is simply covering soil with a protective coating. The advantages of mulching are that it helps kill off existing weeds, prevents new weeds from growing and stops soil erosion.

What to grow.

The number one rule is to grow what you want to eat. There's no point putting the energy and effort into cultivating a field of broad beans if you aren't going to eat them. If you don't have a lot of space, consider growing quick maturing plants. You may love sprouting broccoli but if it takes a year to grow, it may not be the best choice for you.

Consider your space and how to maximise it. If you have a small space, growing a crop of sweet corn isn't a reality, although you could grow potatoes in a container.

If you are new to gardening start by growing a few easy crops and work your way up to more challenging ones. It's less work and more economically viable to grow a few things well, rather than growing lots of things badly.

Some great vegetables for beginners include tomatoes, green dwarf beans, runner beans, mange touts, radish, lettuce and assorted salad leaves (including rocket, mizuna, mibuna and mustard leaves), beetroot, spinach, chard, courgettes and potatoes. Potatoes are great as they are not only delicious but also very satisfying to grow; even in a small area they grow well in a container.

It is tempting to sow a whole packet of seed at once, but bear in mind, for example, that one courgette plant will feed two people easily (and use up a fair bit of space).

Make room for fruit. Fruit such as raspberries, currants, gooseberries and apple trees all require a minimal amount of effort and pruning but will reward you with a good harvest for years.

Don't forget perennials. These are plants that grow back each year, saving you the effort of annual sowing, and include plants like globe artichokes, Jerusalem artichokes and rhubarb.

Now we know what we want to grow we need to prepare our soil ready for planting and get growing! Tanya Sadourian explains what to do next.

You need to decide where in your garden to plant your vegetables. Most vegetables want as much daylight as possible. Choose a sunny - if possible south facing – spot, not shaded by trees, buildings or a fence and close to a water supply if possible (having to carry watering cans endlessly gets boring pretty quickly).

Preparing the plot: soil.

Whether growing in a container or on a vegetable plot, the soil needs to be fertile and well drained. Once you've chosen a plot, you will need to prepare the ground. If it is a large area you would usually hire a rotovator. For smaller areas, once the lawn (if there is any) is lifted, you need to dig it over, starting at one end by digging at least a spade's depth, adding plenty. of well rotted horse manure and/or rotted kitchen or garden compost

This is really important in order to get healthy, productive, happy plants. The soil will be considerably improved and organic matter helps release nitrogen, minerals, and other essential nutrients. Make sure you don't dig when it is too wet. You'll know it's too wet to work if you squeeze a handful of soil and it stays in a ball rather than breaking up.

You also want to make sure you don't compact the soil by treading over it as you turn it (that plank of wood would be handy now!); you want loose, crumbly soil. If you're using raised beds the issue of soil compaction will not be such a concern. Raised beds are very popular nowadays and are good if you have terrible soil. (They are very useful here in the south of England, where we are susceptible to chalky soil!)

Once you've dug over the plot and incorporated the 'organic matter', the plot is prepped.

Spring is planting time. If you get a plot in spring, dig it over and add well rotted farmyard manure. Remove and burn any perennial weeds. If you obtain a new plot in autumn, cover the soil with heavy black plastic or carpet over the winter to kill off any weeds (but consider that carpet may not be allowed to cover an allotment plot). If your beds are weed free, sow 'green manures', for example red clover or mustard. Before flowering, dig the plants back into the soil, as they add a lot of nutrients.

Before sowing seeds direct or planting seedlings you will need to rake or hoe the soil to a fine tilth (a crumbly texture). Make it as even as possible. You may want to mark your planting lines with a piece of string and some wooden sticks.

Sowing your seeds.

People often have their own preferred methods of sowing, for example I always sow my lettuce or salad seedlings in 'cells' or 'modules' which are small individual pots all contained within one tray. Using modules means that seedlings are not disturbed when planted out as they do not have to be split up. They have no competition for nutrients or space and have the potential to be really healthy. You could sow seeds in individual pots - a few seeds per pot - and thin out before planting.

Remember that when handling seedlings, always hold them gently by the leaves and never by the stem.

If sowing in trays or modules, buy some compost and mix with about a third of washed sharp sand (not from a builder's yard as it won't be washed and may contain salt).

When sowing, remember to date and label the seedlings, sow thinly and water using a watering can with a rose.

For sowing directly outside, you need to make sure you are sowing seeds when it is warm enough for them to germinate and grow. If seedlings are planted too early, when it is still cold and there is a risk of a frost, seedlings may die, rot or be 'checked', which means their growth will be massively hindered. By waiting until it is warm enough, plants will do much better. Frost can occur even during May so patience is a real virtue here. As a rule, if, in the spring, it is muddy enough for the soil to stick to your shoes, don't plant.

Getting the most from your crops by Harvest Brighton and Hove and Tanya Sadourian.

- Soil; the single most important thing to remember is your soil. Feed it and look after it; if you keep adding organic matter it will be able to look after your plants.

- If you have beds, use crop rotation and look into companion planting. This will help with reducing attacks from pests and diseases. Crop rotation can be very confusing so keep it as simple as possible. Don't sow or plant anything more than once in the same place for three years. This will help prevent diseases and pests.

- Keep weeding. Vegetables grow best without weed competition so hoe them every week.

- Mulch your beds with compost or a semi-permeable membrane to keep water in and weeds out.

- Hoe your beds regularly to ensure the soil remains in a loose, friable condition so that it can absorb subsequent rainfall.

Water:

- If this is not provided by rainfall, you will need to water your crops yourself. Regular and even watering is the key; uneven watering will lead to tougher vegetables that are more prone to splitting. You do not want plants to wilt or to become too dry but at the same time don't drown them. When they are young, ensure the soil is kept moist.
- Watering daily until plants become established is a good idea.

When they are bigger, most plants can manage with a little less water. If growing in containers, be aware that they will dry out relatively quickly.

- Water the soil not the plant. It is the roots that want to access the water, so ensure you don't just dampen the top of the soil. Morning and evening are the best times to water.
- Once fruit and vegetables have set, regular watering means tasty, tender crops. Tomatoes in particular like regular water and tomato feed, especially once the fruit has set. The best time to water tomatoes is early in the morning (at night it will attract the slugs).

Sowing and picking:

- Keep sowing: after you take out your early potatoes you still have time to sow a second different crop in the same bed. Many crops such as salad, beans, peas, and many greens can be sown in smaller batches over many months, thus avoiding a glut of one vegetable.
- Keep picking; many crops such as raspberries, strawberries, courgettes, and cucumbers need to be picked regularly so that they can keep producing.

Pests and diseases:

- If your first lettuce crop gets eaten by slugs, don't be disheartened. Slugs can be very destructive, but there are organic pellets you can use. Using coarse grit as a collar around the plant also helps to deter them as they don't like to crawl over it. Another way to protect young plants is to surround them with cut plastic bottles, or buy an organic pest control.
- Nematodes feed off snails so will keep your plants safe. You should also water plants in the morning to avoid creating

attractive damp conditions for these pests and pick slugs off your plants in the evenings if you can.

- Spray ants and aphids off your plants with a strong water spray.
- Protect fruit, greens and peas from birds by building or buying a fruit cage.

- Plants want to grow so given the right conditions they will!

What about small spaces? By Hedvig Murray.

Growing your own food is all well and good when you have a garden. But what about if you live in a flat or just have a balcony in the centre of town? You can get growing wherever you are.

In fact there are many advantages of growing in window boxes and in containers: you can choose your soil, there are fewer slugs, you can move the pots, and everything is close to home, which makes it easier to look after.

There is so much information out there, so where do you start? I propose that you start by going through the design process. I find that the permaculture method is the most useful when growing in small spaces because it has developed a straight forward approach to sustainable design. It is easily remembered by the acronym SADIM, which stands for Survey, Assess, Design, Implement and Maintain.

The tools and techniques can be applied to spaces of all different sizes, which is especially useful if you are starting out without a garden. And yes, it really is worth doing a design first; best to make the mistakes on paper.

The first step is to survey. Get yourself a journal and start observing. How big is your space? Pace it out, and draw up a rough plan. How much sun does it get? Take photos and mark on the plan which areas are in sun in the morning, afternoon and early evening. Where does your water come from? If you have containers already, measure the soil depth. These are the most important factors to survey. If you notice other things like which direction the wind comes from, note them down in the journal.

Next assess what could grow in those conditions. This information can be found on the back of seed packets or on the internet. The best things to go for are 'cut and come again' salad leaves, herbs and some edible flowers. They are not expensive to buy, grow quickly and keep coming back. What salad leaves and herbs do you like eating? There's no point growing it if you don't like eating it.

Then start designing by matching the information you have about the plants you want to grow with the conditions in your growing space. What other things happen in your space? Where do you like to sit? Are there animals or insects such as butterflies that you want to encourage to come to your space? Grow the right thing in the right place, and it is more likely to work.

The plants you harvest or need to look after the most need to be really accessible, so put them as close to your door, window or path as you can.

To implement your design, start sowing or get some seedlings, I would encourage you to get organic seeds. They aren't that much more expensive than regular seeds, and you could always buy and share them with friends, or swap them with others. You could also grow heritage seeds (rare and unusual varieties), an easy way to encourage biodiversity in your garden. Then get some good organic compost (or better still, make your own) to transplant them into. Healthy soil results in healthier plants. When maintaining your space remember that when growing in containers and window boxes, you need to be aware that they dry out more quickly and need regular feeding with a liquid feed, which you can make yourself.

There are lots of things you can grow. If you look at our website you can find out what other people have grown on their balconies. It is best to start out small and succeed rather than be disappointed because you have tried to grow too much. Then if you get matched with Grow Your Neighbour's Own or obtain part of an allotment, you can grow other larger plants.

Some things won't work out, but don't let that get you down - it happens to everyone. Just make sure you take note of how things are going. Take lots of photos or write down observations - you'll thank yourself next year.

Many people are deterred from growing their own food due to lack of space or long allotment queues. If you have enough time and you want to grow more than can fit on your window sill, Chris Callard from Brighton and Hove initiative Grow Your Neighbour's Own can help! He explains why a little technicality such as lack of space shouldn't stop you...

Grow Your Neighbour's Own garden share scheme by Chris Callard.

Been waiting for years on allotment waiting lists? Ever seen an unused garden or plot of land and wished you could grow your own food there? Or do you have a garden or area of land on which you'd love to see food grown? If you live in Brighton and Hove, Grow Your Neighbour's Own garden share scheme want to help remedy the situation...

There are many residents of Brighton and Hove who don't have gardens but would like to grow their own food. There are over a thousand people on allotment waiting lists, and although the lists have recently reopened this still means a long wait. Many other residents have gardens but are not able to grow food, whether for lack of time, knowledge or mobility. There are also areas of land around blocks of flats, community buildings, and many other places that could be used for growing food. Grow Your Neighbour's Own is about pairing up gardeners with garden- and land-owners. The scheme wants to help form lasting (gardening) relationships between local people. The garden- or land-owner and gardener arrange between them what they will grow and how often the gardening will take place, sharing the produce as it is harvested.

There are additional benefits of growing food in someone else's garden: getting to know more people in your neighbourhood; and bringing people from different generations into contact where there had not previously been an opportunity to do so.

The pairing scheme is for anyone who lives in the city: owners with gardens or land of any size, and gardeners of all levels of experience. It tries to pair up people with similar expectations. It is also for people who currently have an allotment but are finding it hard to maintain, and would like to find a co-worker with whom to share the load.

Grow Your Neighbour's Own and Transition Towns.

The garden share scheme grew out of the Transition Town network, a nationwide organisation which encourages community responses to the challenges of climate change and peak oil. Although the scheme is primarily about allowing more people to grow their own food, it is also a drive to see more locally produced food, and as such reducing food miles in order to bring down carbon emissions in the effort to combat climate change. Furthermore, by producing more of our own food we help the city to be more resilient to the effects of rising energy prices and dwindling energy supplies.

A few frequently asked questions about Grow Your Neighbour's Own.

Do I have to pay to be part of the scheme?

The scheme is run by volunteers and it costs nothing to be matched up with a garden-owner or gardener.

Who provides and pays for tools, seeds, materials and so on?

These and other questions will be discussed by the gardener and owner before growing starts, but generally it will be expected that the gardener will pay for the materials.

Do you check for references from gardeners?

The scheme asks for a personal reference from all gardeners. In addition we understand that some garden-owners may be a little wary of letting someone they don't know into their house (especially the elderly and more vulnerable). We will offer the possibility of matching a garden-owner with a gardener who has a current CRB check if required, but this will limit the choice of gardeners you might be matched with. As a gardener, if you already have a current CRB check, you'll have more choice of gardens!

What if I'm not happy with the way things are working out?

The scheme is always there to help if you feel things are not working out as you expected. We hope that any minor problems will be sorted out between garden-owner and gardener

You do, however, have the option of withdrawing yourself from the scheme, or asking for another pairing.

How to join the scheme.

Find a nearby garden-owner yourself! You don't need Grow Your Neighbour's Own to start growing food. If you know a neighbour who has a garden or plot of land but who can't grow food for whatever reason, go and introduce yourself and suggest the idea! You can have a look at the guidelines on our website for growing in someone else's garden if you need to, and our growing links for how to go about it.

Register your details with Grow Your Neighbour's Own.

Register with the scheme on the website (www.growyour-neighboursown.org.uk) or you can phone our office at the Brighton & Hove Food Partnership on 01273 431700 to register your details and we'll tell you more about the scheme. Once you have registered there won't necessarily be a match for you straight away; we want to make good matches by location and expectations from the scheme, so there may not be someone who immediately fits the bill. If we don't find you a match straight away we will keep you updated from time to time to let you know we haven't forgotten about you!

With thanks to:

Jess Crocker, Sarah Walters and Ann Baldridge from Harvest Brighton and Hove.

Jess Crocker is the Harvest Manager who is responsible for the overall delivery of the project as well as marketing, communications and media work.

Sarah Waters is the Harvest Growing Officer for the Food Partnership; and Ann Baldridge is the Development Officer for Harvest Brighton and Hove.

Harvest Brighton and Hove is part of The Brighton and Hove Food Partnership, a membership organisation that is working towards a sustainable food system for Brighton & Hove. They believe that healthy people make a healthy city and that all residents should be able to enjoy food that is nutritious and produced in ways that respect the environment, animals and people.
They undertake lobbying work and provide training and information to achieve:
- better access to affordable fresh, seasonal food
- more locally produced food
- more opportunities to learn to cook and grow food
- a better understanding of the links between food and health
- a better understanding of where food comes from. Their projects include community cookery, healthy weight service, school food work and Harvest Brighton & Hove.

http://www.bhfood.org.uk

Tanya Sadourian is Transition Town's very own veg doctor and has a great deal of experience in growing vegetables and organic gardening. She has worked as a home economist, caterer, teacher and recipe writer, all the time continuing to garden and grow, both in the UK and in the very different climate of sub-tropical Australia. Tanya has been involved in setting up organic kitchen gardens with school children in the UK and Australia and doing more work in food education recently, she has been teaching adults to grow and cook healthy foods.

Hedvig Murray set up Get Growing, a social enterprise that trains people to grow food in their own homes using organic methods and permaculture design. She has years of experience in growing food in her own garden, working on organic farms and for veg box schemes. She is a certified permaculture designer, and is aiming to complete her permaculture diploma by the end of 2010.
hedvig@getgrowing.org.uk www.getgrowing.org.uk

Chris Callard. Inspired by other garden share schemes around the country, Chris Callard started up Grow Your Neighbour's Own in Brighton & Hove at the end of 2008.
www.growyourneighboursown.org.uk

Section 4) Transport

Transportation is unavoidable. We need to get from A to B. Whether A to B is from one side of town to another or to the other side of the world, somehow we need to get there. However, the vast majority of us travel by car and often short distances or on our own. Imagine eight forty five am in your local neighbourhood; the dreaded school run. Think Friday at five pm on the A27 through Worthing and picture a gorgeous sunny summer morning on the A23 coming into Brighton. The roads of Sussex like many throughout the UK are often congested; consider the amount of cars on our roads and the consequential amount of pollution that this causes. We rely on motor vehicles and it could be argued that we overuse them. The question is what are the alternatives? How can we reduce our reliance on the automobile and still get from A to B?

Why we should leave the car at home by Lucie Britsch.

We used to think the future of cars was faster, high-tech, even flying vehicles, but the reality is that the future of the car now has an agenda and that agenda is green. We still want faster, more advanced, vehicles but we want them to address the changing needs of our planet and lives.

Our world is undeniably automobile-dominated. There are a huge amount of roads on our planet.

We need to act now. Climate change is a very real threat that is already upon us. Furthermore, with insecure oil supplies the need to find a sustainable alternative to the private automobile is more urgent now than ever.

Why we love our cars.

Our cars are often much more than just a means of getting from A to B. We take pride in our cars. We feed them, clean them, some people even name them. Depending on how much time we spend in them and how much travelling we do they are extensions of our homes or our offices. We love our cars. They are a sign of freedom. Since they first went into mass production in the late nineteenth century and roads started to be built they have given us a new sense of freedom and endless opportunity.

But this love affair is having a terrible affect on our planet and it is more important now than ever that we learn to be less reliant on our cars, or ideally not rely on them at all. This is a huge challenge because we have become so dependent on them.

Why we should not rely on cars.

- In the UK transportation produces an estimated twenty five per cent of our total greenhouse gas emissions.[1]

---

1   Crown Copyright: http://www.decc.gov.uk/en/content/cms/statistics/climate_change/gg_emissions/uk_emissions/2009_prov/2009_prov.aspx

- Walking and cycling produce no direct greenhouse emissions.
- Public transport produces lower emissions per passenger than cars.
- As I write this petrol prices in Sussex are at one pound nineteen pence per litre and they have been even higher than this.
- There is only a finite amount of oil and eventually it will run out. How will we run our cars when it does?
- Emissions for private transport are far higher than emissions produced by public transport. This is a trend that is reflected in data from 1997 to 2007.[1]

We need to find another, renewable and sustainable, source of fuel or give up our cars completely. Before it's too late.

Car emissions are a leading cause of the greenhouse effect and of climate change. Every time you get behind the wheel you are contributing to the demise of our planet. Harsh, but true.

Although car pollution has significantly decreased over the last twenty years, due to a changes from leaded to unleaded gasoline and changes made by car manufacturers we still have a long way to go.

Transport accounts for an estimated twenty eight per cent of the total UK emissions of carbon dioxide (CO_2),[2] the major contributor to climate change. Carbon dioxide is thought to contribute greatly to global warming. Carbon dioxide is necessary for plants, that convert it to oxygen, but in high concentrations contributes to the greenhouse effect. Aside from CO_2

1   Crown Copyright: http://www.dft.gov.uk/pgr/statistics/datatablespublications/tsgb/2009edition/section3energyenvironment.pdf
2   Crown Copyright: http://www.decc.gov.uk/en/content/cms/statistics/climate_change/gg_emissions/uk_emissions/2009_prov/2009_prov.aspx

production, car pollution affects the environment in a number of different ways. From noise pollution, air pollution to water pollution; car pollution impacts upon the environment on a large level.

Reducing CO2 emissions.

The EU is working to reduce CO2 emissions from new cars. They believe that it is important for customers to be more aware of the CO2 emissions from vehicles that they are contemplating buying.[1] Colour-coded labels, similar to those used on washing machines and fridges, are now frequently displayed in car showrooms explaining how much CO2 new models emit and the running costs of the vehicle over 12000 miles.[2] However, as traffic levels are predicted to increase, road transport will continue to be a significant contributor to greenhouse gas emissions.

Air pollution.

Air pollution is a major problem that arises from our reliance on the motor car. Although in the past air pollution has been more likely to be caused by the burning of fossil fuels, such as coal, it is now commonly caused by cars.[3] Air pollutants from transport include nitrogen oxides, fine particles, carbon monoxide and volatile organic compounds including benzene and

1   http://ec.europa.eu/environment/air/transport/co2/co2_cars_labelling.htm
2   Crown Copyright: http://actonco2.direct.gov.uk/actonco2/home/what-you-can-do/ Out-shopping/buying-your-car.html#b4
3   Crown Copyright: http://www.direct.gov.uk/en/Environmentandgreenerliving/ Thewiderenvironment/Pollution/DG_180281

1,3-butadiene. All have a damaging impact on the health of people, animals and plant life. In towns and alongside busy roads, vehicles are responsible for much of local air pollution.[1] Although new technology and cleaner fuel formulations will continue to cut emissions of pollutants, the increasing number of vehicles on the road and the amount of miles driven is eroding these benefits.

Noise pollution.

Although many people do not consider it a pollutant, noise from private and public automobiles, aeroplanes and trains can all cause hearing problems and disturbance. Noise is still a form of pollution and can have detrimental effects on our environment and general health and well-being.

Noise from road traffic affects a vast number of people in the UK. Sources include engine noise, heavy vehicles, tyre noise, car horns, car stereos, door slamming, and squeaking brakes. Low noise road surfaces, effective noise barriers in sensitive locations, and low noise tyres can all help reduce noise levels and encouraging people to close car windows when playing loud music would also significantly reduce the impact of noise.

1   http://www.airquality.co.uk/what_causes.php?n_action=pollutants&item=4

What can you do to reduce your greenhouse gas emissions from transport?

If you really cannot bear to leave your car at home all of the time there are a number of things you can do to minimise your impact and reduce your carbon footprint. You should regularly aim to do the following:

- Avoid using cars for short journeys, combine trips or, alternatively, walk, cycle, or take a bus.

- Care for your vehicle; check tuning, tyre pressure, brakes and fuel consumption. Regular servicing helps keep your car efficient and saves fuel.

- Lighten up! Roof racks add drag and other unnecessary weight as well as increasing fuel consumption.

- When your tyres need replacing consider low rolling resistance replacements; ask your tyre fitter for advice.

- Drive gently; racing starts and sudden stops increase fuel consumption. Use higher gears when traffic conditions allow.

- Keep your driving speed to below seventy mph (miles per hour); peak fuel efficiency is at around fifty five mph for most cars, driving at eighty mph dramatically reduces fuel efficiency

- Switch off when stationary. If you are stuck in traffic or stopping for longer than a minute switch off your engine. Idling engines make sitting in jams even more unpleasant. Do not run the engine unnecessarily; drive off soon after starting.

- Be considerate of those around you, reduce the volume of your car stereo or close your car window in residential areas, and avoid sounding your horn or revving your engine.

- Refrain from using air conditioning and on board electrical devices. These increase fuel consumption.

- Investigate alternatives. If you're looking for a new car there are a number of different technologies and fuels available. Existing cars can also be adapted to give off lower emissions.

- Not travelling! The internet and improvements in information technology mean you can work, shop, talk, do practically anything, from your own home. Offices are also becoming more tolerant about employees working from home one or two days a week.

- If you really have to buy a new car then select a more fuel-efficient vehicle simply by electing the smallest, most carbon-efficient car. However, consider the energy used and the green house gases emitted during the production of the vehicle in the first place.

These small changes can have a big impact our quest to combat climate change and if everyone did them there would be hope for the future of our planet. If you can only do some of them or inspire others to do the same, it's a start in the right direction.

To explain a little more about the alternatives to private transport that a lot of us do not even contemplate we hear from Joe Markendale and Ellie Cooley with some advice.

Alternative modes of transport by Joe Markendale and Ellie Cooley.

In this section we will take a brief look at the main alternatives available to private vehicle use in Sussex:

Car sharing.

For those of us who have become accustomed to car travel and desire it over other methods of public transport, car sharing schemes provide an opportunity to collectively use cars in a cheaper and more energy-efficient way. Car sharing not only lessens the number of unoccupied places, but also allows individuals to make equal distance journeys at a greatly reduced cost. In terms of emissions, the main advantage here is that passenger's carbon footprints are significantly diminished through sharing the car's emissions. Compared with passengers travelling in their own vehicles, car sharing is a vastly greener and more efficient mode of transport. It follows, then, that one major environmental benefit of the increasing trend in car sharing is the resulting reduction in privately used vehicles in operation. This reduces the UK's gross emissions as well as limiting the other impacts of motor vehicles on the environment. For those areas in which they do not already operate, organising local community car sharing schemes need not take too much time or effort, merely connecting fellow travellers through local advertisements and word of mouth may be all that's necessary. Check with your employers to see if they already offer a car sharing scheme and if they don't why not get together with your colleagues and set one up?

Alternatively, here are some existing schemes in Sussex:

www.catcharide.co.uk - this website provides the opportunity for drivers and passengers to offer and request shared journeys online.

www.travelchoice.org - another online service for connecting drivers and passengers.

Buses and Coaches.

Making use of public buses and coaches hugely reduces environmental pollution and atmospheric degradation. Our carbon footprints are massively reduced when we use these modes of transport as the fuel and emissions are spread across all of the passengers. Much like car sharing; buses and coaches are at their most energy-efficient when they are full of people. Other advantages include the minimisation of traffic congestion, the reduced financial cost of fuel and parking, and the regular physical exercise of walking to the bus stop. With some buses and coaches now running on fuels much lower in CO2 emissions such as liquefied petroleum gas (LPG) and bio diesel, the future of bus and coach service in the UK is brighter and greener than ever before.

Trains.

Trains are another form of public transport which, when used, can reduce our impact on the environment. Powered either by diesel or petrol, the UK's trains facilitate reasonably fast travel virtually anywhere in Britain. Trains' emissions and energy use are again spread over the total number of passengers, making them far more energy-efficient than cars.

Many of the UK's trains now incorporate a regenerative braking system that converts kinetic energy generated by the moving train back into the train system.[1] Regenerative braking is more energy-efficient than traditional braking, in which the kinetic energy of the train is instead released as heat and ultimately wasted.

Summary.

Listed below are the volumes of CO_2 produced by trains, buses, and private motor vehicles domestically per year: (figures from 2007)

Trains: 3.85 million tonnes
Buses: 3.02 million tonnes
Cars: 77.10 million tonnes

This means that trains account for three per cent of our transport CO_2 emissions, buses for two per cent and cars produce fifty eight per cent of our CO_2 produced by transport.[2] The rest of the emissions are caused by alternative modes of transport.

---

1   http://www.southernrailway.com/southern/our-corporate-responsibility/environ
ment/
2   Crown Copyright: 2007: http://actonco2.direct.gov.uk/actonco2/home/what-you-
can-do/On-the-move/Compare-CO2-emissions.html

The figures show that emissions produced by cars are much higher than that of trains and buses combined. Travelling by car not only significantly increases one's carbon footprint but also often costs more per journey than other methods. Completely carbon neutral modes of transport such as walking and cycling obviously have the least negative impact on the environment and are, therefore, by far the most green and healthy as they provide us with a regular source of physical exercise. For environmentally conscious travellers; buses, coaches and trains are more environmentally friendly than private automobiles.

A gradual reduction in privately owned vehicles in the UK would lead to a situation in which there is less pollution in urban areas, less disruption of ecosystems, and a greater sense of peacefulness in our communities. The current increase in the popularity of cycling and walking over driving, steadily decreases our environmental pollution, whilst simultaneously connecting us to our natural habitats. Through personally nurturing this connection we might finally begin to understand how our lifestyles affect the environment.

One final point to note, as we scrutinise and compare the efficiency of different modes of transport, is that as functioning individuals in society, we must strive to find ways of travelling that are both practical and suitable for us without getting so bogged down with the details that we actually don't end up travelling in a greener way at all. Any choice we make towards a greener mode of transport is a positive one whether it's sharing a car, catching the bus, riding the train, cycling or walking. We must make the decisions we can, when we can to gradually reduce our carbon footprint whilst still maintaining and improving our lives. When approached in this way, making the transition to a greener way of life is an enjoyable process that enhances our lives rather than limits them.

Later in the book we discuss alternative fuels as a solution to the finite supply of fossil fuels and more specifically we mention the use of bio diesel as a sustainable fuel that can be used in a standard diesel vehicle. The Big Lemon is a bus company based in Brighton and Hove who run on biodiesel. We hear from Tom Druitt, the brains behind the Lemon to find out how the Big Lemon are doing their bit for the environment.

Sustainable Transport – The Big Lemon Story by Tom Druitt.

Human beings are strange creatures. Faced with overwhelming evidence that we need to change the way we live in order to survive on this planet, we still seem reluctant to do so. There are many reasons for this, but three stand out immediately. One is the fact that although the importance of the problem is well known, most of us do not experience the immediate urgency of the problem on a daily basis. The ones who do are often in the least powerful position to do anything about it. Another is that there appear to be rewards today for inaction (unfettered economic growth, foreign holidays and so on), where as the rewards for action (survival of our habitat and ultimately of our species) seem a long way off, and many of the people who benefit from inaction today will not be around to pay the price tomorrow. The third reason is responsibility; whose responsibility is it?

In this article we will look at a local, practical solution to the problem of climate change. It is not a revolutionary idea or a new technology, just a simple, community-based approach to cutting carbon dioxide emissions through transport. The project is known as The Big Lemon, and its aim is to develop the most sustainable mode of transport within a community.

As a teenager living in a rural area of Sussex I had long been frustrated with the inadequacies of public transport. I was particularly annoyed that our village once had a railway station but that this was removed before I was born, and now the only option was an infrequent bus service with poor customer service, little information and quite frankly few reasons as to why anyone would be tempted to use it. As an adult going back to visit my parents I saw little had changed, I kept thinking, 'there must be a better way... if we are serious about reducing car use, pollution, congestion and ultimately global warming, we must be able to offer people a better alternative.'

I left my job and got to work. When I had the outline of a plan, I organised a public meeting in a Brighton pub and presented my idea to the fifteen or so people who turned up, with a discussion afterwards covering all sorts of topics from the role of public transport in combating climate change to the lack of buses from Hove railway station to the seafront. The best thing to come out of the meeting, however, was all the new contacts assembled, and an offer from an ex-bus driver to drive the first four days of our first service for free.

On the 1st September 2007 The Big Lemon launched its first bus service, a limited-stop express service between Brighton railway station and Falmer. The hallmarks of the service were eco friendliness, good customer service and value for money. The buses all ran on waste cooking oil from local restaurants, as I felt it was important to practice what we preached and try and run the operation in the most sustainable way possible. The importance of good customer service was obvious too; if people enjoyed themselves on our buses they would use them again; if they didn't, they wouldn't. And as for the price, if we were serious about encouraging as many people as possible to use the service, we had to charge the absolute minimum. Bus prices in Brighton and Hove had been creeping up significantly, and this was

was pricing some people out of the market as well as making cars seem more competitive than before. This was something we had to try and stop.

Some people criticised our choice of route, pointing out that there were already lots of buses serving it, but there were a number of reasons for starting with that particular one.

Falmer is home to two universities, the students of which had recently staged a demonstration on the buses against fare increases, and so they seemed the perfect audience. Students also tend to be thirsty for change, interested in new things, environmentally-aware and skint. All these factors worked in our favour. But the most important reason for this choice was that the universities were distinct communities, communities we could engage with, build a relationship with and learn to serve their travel needs in the most efficient way.

The service was very well received by those who used it, but unfortunately this turned out not to be enough to sustain it. There were a number of reasons for this. As much as people liked it, it was not frequent enough as it only ran every half hour, it did not fit in well with lecture times, and as a limited stop service it did not stop at all the stops.

After two months we managed to change the service registration to run at different times and stop at every stop, but it was too late. We were running out of money very quickly and did not have enough to give the adapted service a fair chance. I called all the staff to the most horrible meeting I had ever had, and told everyone that we had enough money to pay wages for one more month, and then we would have to de-register the service and make everyone redundant.

However, we never made it to the end of that month as staff lost confidence and left, and by the end of the week the service collapsed.

What followed was very messy indeed, as we battled to save the business. We had very little cash left, huge debts and a regulatory nightmare to deal with as we'd had to cancel the service without giving the required notice to the Traffic Commissioner. But worst of all, we had let our passengers down, and all those people who had supported us and believed in the project. I felt so depressed that I found it hard to get up in the mornings.

The New Year, however, brought new energy and a stubborn determination to make it work. We still had one of the original drivers and a lot of support, and so we registered a slimmed-down service with one bus running hourly, and built it up gradually from there. We were lucky enough to have a hard-core following of passengers who kept using the service not due to convenience, but because they believed in it and wanted to support it. Gradually the word got around and more and more people started using it, and the service grew steadily from there, quickly becoming the transport of choice for a large number of students. The next couple of years also saw huge growth in private hire services and music festival coaches, and in 2009 we were the 8th fastest growing social business in the RBS SE 100 Index, an index of UK social businesses.

The question to consider is; why do our passengers use us? We quickly developed a reputation as a friendly bus company, and we insist that all our drivers greet people as they get on, and acknowledge them as they leave. We have a commitment to sustainability and affordability, and charge the absolute minimum we can manage. We sometimes mess up, but all our customers know we do our best, and if we ever let them down, we listen to them, apologise and make it up to them. However, if you ask anyone what we're about, they will tell you that it's all about cooking oil.

The Big Lemon was the first bus company in the UK to run its whole fleet on 100 per cent biodiesel from locally-sourced waste cooking oil. The oil is collected from hotels, restaurants, takeaways and school kitchens around Sussex. It then goes through a three-stage process to turn it into biodiesel. First all the leftover chips and all traces of water are removed (if there's any water left, the process which follows ends up producing soap instead of biodiesel), and then the pure waste oil undergoes a chemical process (transesterification) with sodium hydroxide and methanol which produces biodiesel (an ester) and glycerine (a by-product which can also be used industrially). Finally the glycerine and biodiesel are separated in a settling tank and piped out into containers ready for use.

Throughout the process the carbon footprint is minimised. The van that collects the waste oil runs on biodiesel; the processing plant's only power source is from a biodiesel-powered generator, and there is no water used in the process apart from to make the tea.

There are many benefits to using biodiesel. As a waste product, if it was not used resourcefully it would either be poured down the drain, polluting the water cycle and solidifying on the sides of sewers until someone spends a lot of money cleaning it off; or it would be sent to landfill. Using this waste product as a fuel reduces our dependence on oil. As a local resource, the energy used in collection, production and delivery locally is a fraction of the energy used to drill for oil, ship it across the world, refine it and deliver it to petrol stations across the country. When it's burnt in an engine, biodiesel produces far less pollution, and as biodiesel comes from plants, all the CO_2 released is no more than the CO_2 taken out of the atmosphere by the plants when they were growing. These benefits are now becoming more and more widely recognised and in the future an increasing number of people will be using biodiesel to power all sorts of things.

So what does the future hold for The Big Lemon? Over the short time we have been running buses, we have gained a lot of experience of running a small, sustainable, community-based public transport service on a very small budget, and we believe that this is where the future lies. It is simply inconceivable that we continue to take individual car ownership for granted, and yet sustainable alternatives are not yet in place on a national scale. We also believe that small is the new big, that the future lies in bespoke solutions tailored to individual communities.

It is with this in mind that we have developed our members' club concept, which in theory means that anyone, anywhere, can use our experience to start their own local sustainable transport solution in their own community. All they need to do is to start a club in their area, recruit as many members as possible and develop an idea, through their members travel needs, as to what kind of service(s) they need in their community. When they have an idea, the cost of providing the service can be calculated, and members can decide how much they would be willing to pay for unlimited use of the service for a year.

Local businesses and other organisations can also get involved, and when the total amount that people have pledged for a year's travel gets to the point where it covers the running costs for a year, the club comes of age, collects the money and with our help and support either starts their own little transport operation to run it, or contracts it to an existing local operator who agrees to run it along the same lines of community, sustainability and good service. The Big Lemon has no ambition to be the next big company to float on the stock market, but if we can help develop lots of off-shoots which take the best of our experience and make it work locally in their area, we will have succeeded in our ambitions. Public transport is not seen as something we can change in our communities, but this needs to change. Anyone can, with the right training and resources, start a bus company. People need to know this. If they are not happy with provision in their community, they can do it themselves. And I'll bet they can do it better than most established bus companies.

What does this mean for you? Anything you want. One day you may decide you want to start a club in your area to start to develop sustainable, affordable transport for your own sustainable, community bus service. In the meantime, there are a number of things you can do, many of which you can do right now:

1. Put this number in your phone: 0871 200 22 33. It is the Traveline and it will give you information on buses, trains and National Express coaches. The South East call centre is open from 0700 to 2200. You can also find them online at www.traveline.info. It's worth having National Rail Enquiries number too (08457 484950) although this is obviously just for trains!

2. Print your local bus and train timetables and put them on your kitchen notice-board or on your fridge so they are always at hand.

3. Stop using out-of-town shopping centres. These centres encourage a car culture because often that's the only way to get to them.

4. Buy a bike. As I write this, there's a folding bike about to be sold on eBay for fifty pounds, and a nice looking mountain bike for fifty eight pounds. Ask your local council what plans they have to improve infrastructure for cyclists.

5. Whenever you see a leaflet or website with 'how to get here' written on it, make sure public transport details are prominent, clear and preferably before the car option. If they are not email the person concerned and suggest they put up clear information on public transport, pointing out the benefits to them (less people using the car park, fewer complaints from neighbours and so on).

6. Have a look at www.thebiglemon.com and see how your community can benefit from a sustainable transport solution.

In order to combat climate change and ensure future generations have a future to look forward to, we must change the way we live very quickly. This does not mean we have to live in a cave and eat shrubs, it just means we have to alter our lifestyles. The great thing about us as humans is that we do not simply have to accept our fate and adapt to it; we actually have the capability to change it. So what are we waiting for, let's do it.

If you still feel the need to drive a car or need one very occasionally, there is an alternative to owning your own vehicle...City Car Club; hourly car and van rental on your doorstep!

City Car Club gives you access to a car, without the hassle and expense of owning one. City Car Club cars are available twenty four hours a day, seven days a week and can be booked by the hour, day, or for as long as you want. The cars are conveniently located in designated parking bays near to where you live and work and can be booked online or by phone in advance, or at the last minute.

City Car Club take care of insurance, tax, servicing, parking permits and even cleaning, so all you need to worry about is enjoying your journey. Members gain access to the cars with their own smart-enabled membership card, which when swiped on the windscreen, unlocks the car. As a member of City Car Club you have access to literally hundreds of cars and vans across the UK.

And it's good for the environment too. Independent research shows that an average of twenty five private cars are taken off the road for every City Car. This is because new members often sell their own car or defer buying one. In addition, surveys show that car club members think more carefully about each trip they make in a car, and make greater use of alternative travel options such as cycling, public transport and walking. And City Car Club have a strict low-emissions policy on fleet selection; as such, City Cars emit thirty seven per cent less CO_2 than those they replace.

For more information go to www.citycarclub.co.uk

With Thanks to:

Lucie Britsch
Has a degree in English and culture and is currently working on her first novel and various non-fiction projects. She is passionate about books, reading and green issues and hopes projects like this will inspire others. She generally likes animals more than humans, unless they're zombies, vampires or werewolves. She currently works in ebooks but dreams of working with real books.

Joe Markendale and Ellie Cooley.

Tom Druitt and The Big Lemon.
Tom Druitt was born in Gloucestershire in 1978 and grew up in Sussex. He was educated at Michael Hall School in Forest Row, and then at Stirling University, where he graduated in Politics, Philosophy and Economics in 2002. Following University Druitt was commissioned at the Royal Military Academy, Sandhurst, and then moved back to Sussex to start a new life in Brighton.

Druitt has always been a regular user of public transport, and gradually became increasingly frustrated with the inability of public transport to provide a viable solution to the nation's transport needs and the challenge of climate change. This prompted him to begin gathering ideas for a new type of bus company, and so The Big Lemon was born. With no prior industry knowledge or experience, this was a project driven by customer experience, and the concept quickly became popular. The Big Lemon was the first bus company in the UK to run all its vehicles on 100 per cent biodiesel from locally-sourced waste cooking oil, and won the Dandelion Award for sustainable business in 2009.

Section 5) Waste and Recycling

The majority of us in Sussex will be aware that we are entitled to a recycling box from our local Council or that we can pay for our recycling to be collected by one of the many organisations that offer this service.

Perhaps you are like me? I rinse out my cat food tins and put them in the trusty black box from my local council, I put all my old newspapers and magazines in a neat stack and all my empty glass jars and bottles out ready for the recycling collectors.

Recycling has become such a hot topic over the last few years that most of us will now recycle obvious materials such as paper and glass automatically, almost as second nature, therefore, I am not going to give you a simple overview about how to recycle, it is the 21st century after all, we all know the basics. It is time instead to think outside of the box and consider what we can do to reduce the amount of waste we produce in the first place and how we can reuse and recycle in innovative and exciting ways.

Sussex waste by David Ackroyd.

In the UK we have heard about the mounting problems associated with the excesses of our consumerism and the mantra of 'our throwaway society' countless times. However, we quite often choose not to investigate what this really means or what we might be able to do about it. Scratch the surface and our fears are realised when the UK waste statistics are revealed to us and we visualise what they mean.

In the UK we throw away around twenty eight million tons of waste per year from households, this amounts to around half a ton of waste per person per year. In recent years this figure has been reducing. In 2008/2009 we saw just over a four per cent reduction from 28.5 million tons in 2007/2008 to 27.3 million tons. And over the preceding five years we've seen a reduction of 1.2 percent annually.[1] This shows that things are moving in the right direction. People are taking notice. The problem is that the volume of waste is just so high. At current levels we in the UK produce enough waste to fill the Albert Hall every two hours, and in Sussex it has been suggested that we throw away enough to fill a local swimming pool every ninety minutes.[2]

This level of waste creation not only provides logistical problems in terms of how we store our waste, treat it and recycle it, but it also puts a massive dent in the public purse. At a cost of fifty pence per person per week, for us in Sussex, waste consumes around thirty nine million pounds per year, a proportion which could be spent elsewhere. Consider this financial impact aside from the environmental cost; it still makes the case for waste reduction.[3]

We are also a growing country. The population is forecast to rise to around seventy million by 2030 according to the Office of National Statistics[4] making the incentive to develop more efficient ways of living never greater.

1   Crown Copyright: Defra, Statistical Release, Ref: 257/09, 5 November 2009: http://www.defra.gov.uk/news/2009/091105a.htm
2   Copyright: East Sussex County Council, Rethink Rubish, http://www.eastsussex.gov.uk/NR/rdonlyres/BE40ADC8-41FD-4868-A019-
3   Copyright: Environmental Services Association, as 2
4   Crown Copyright: Office for National Statistics, Statistical Bulletin, 21 October 2009: http://www.statistics.gov.uk/pdfdir/pproj1009.pdf

As it stands today around half of all our waste goes to landfill.[1] In the south east we fare slightly better than the national average of fifty per cent of waste sent to landfill by sending forty six per cent. In this last decade we have come a long way from the eighty per cent we deposited to landfill across the country in 2001, however, we in the south east still have a way to go to match the work done in the West Midlands where only just over thirty two per cent of municipal waste now ends its life filling up our countryside.[2]

The problems with landfill are vast and varied. We all know how terribly smelly, dusty, noisy, fly-infested places they are to live next to with many residents living nearby unwilling to open windows for the obvious consequences that materialise. Moreover, it seems that house prices can suffer too. A Defra study found that those houses which lay within half a mile of landfill sites could expect to be worth on average 5,500 pounds less than a similar property elsewhere.[3]

1   Crown Copyright: Defra, Statistical Release, Ref: 257/09, 5 November 2009: http://www.defra.gov.uk/news/2009/091105a.htm
2   Crown Copyright: Defra, Municipal Waste Statistics, November 2009: http://www.defra.gov.uk/evidence/statistics/environment/wastats/index.htm
3   Crown Copyright: Defra, 'A study to estimate the disamenity costs of landfill inGreat Britain', 2003, http://www.defra.gov.uk/environment/waste/strategy/legislation/landfill/documents/landfill_disamenity.pdf

With landfill sites filling up around the country there is pressure on every council to find new sites. But nobody wants a landfill site near their back yard and cries of 'NIMBYISM' can be heard every time a site close to residents is proposed. It really is our problem. We are the ones creating these fly-infested smelly pits and it is our responsibility to reduce, recycle and reuse as much as we possibly can.

The rotting waste of landfills produce huge amounts of methane gas in the magnitude of two million tons per year. Methane is a by-product that is twenty times more damaging as a green house gas than $CO2$.[1] Thankfully our ability to capture the methane released from landfills is improving and might provide a viable source of energy that we could convert to heat or electricity. The other main way of dealing with non-recyclable waste is incineration. Here too we can produce heat and electricity which go some way to providing a useful energy source. This method is known as Energy from Waste (EfW), and currently all of our waste that is incinerate (fifteen per cent) in the South East produces energy.[2] It is far from determined which method – EfW or methane capture from landfill – is better for our environment, but the issue for us does not change: the less waste we produce the less green house gases (GHG) we produce.

The refrain remains the same; reduce, reuse, recycle. And it is in that order. If we start by reducing what we obtain then we eliminate the energy used in the production and transportation of those items. Next, having obtained items we need to ask ourselves how can we reuse them in some way or other? Or, can someone else reuse them? There is a difference between reusing something and

1   Copyright: Environment Agency, 'Limiting Climate Change: Landfill Gas', http://www.grdp.org/static/documents/Research/%2814%29_Landfill_mitigati on_FINAL.pdf
2   Crown Copyright: Defra, Municipal Waste Statistics, November 2009: http://www.defra.gov.uk/evidence/statistics/environment/wastats/index.htm

recycling something. Recycling can be quite energy costly when compared to reducing and reusing as the material to be recycled needs collecting, transporting, treating, and feeding back into industrial processes.

There are a great many ways in which we can reduce our waste, and a near infinite number of people and organisations advising us to do so. The main theme of reducing our waste, as with all changes in habit, is to find ways that help us continually think about our actions. This way every decision we process is mediated through, what we might call in this case, a 'waste-reduction filter!' To get some ideas flowing I've selected some of the main, easy interventions than can help make a difference to the amount of waste we create:

- Planning meals, by knowing what we want to eat over the course of a week enables us to make more precise decisions when purchasing and helps us to avoid throwing away unused food.

- Stock taking, every shop or restaurant has to do a stock take and for the domestic god or goddess knowing what we have in the fridge-freezer or on the spice shelf can help us avoid doubling up on things we have forgotten we already have, help us use what we've already got, and inspire us to more creative cooking!

- Serving sizes, why cook more than you can eat? When preparing meals think about who is dining and what size portion they are likely to finish. It is better to be on the conservative size especially if you're planning a dessert. And even if you're not, better to let the meal digest a little, you may find you've eaten enough anyway. On the odd occasion you have leftovers why not think about this as a meal for tomorrow's lunch, or freeze it to be eaten another day?

- Compost your waste, home composting is a great way to avoid our reliance on large infrastructure and highly centralised waste systems.[1] Not only does home composting reduce energy and therefore provide environmental savings, it will provide you with a rich source of energy for growing your own vegetables and salads. A surprisingly large amount of our waste can be composted, consider for a minute how much of your own waste can be composted. There are a number of ways we can compost our household waste, from a small wormery, a kitchen sized compost bin, to a fully fledged outdoor compost heap, and we can buy these at discounted rates from our local councils from as little as twenty pounds for a kitchen compost bin. Composting is quite often perceived to require a great deal of effort, space and time to provide anything useful at all. But this is not necessarily the case. As Elliot Coleman says, 'compost wants to happen',[2] and with a few hints and tips we can speed up this natural process so that we create compost as fast as possible. There are a great many resources when it comes to helping us compost and one of the best for getting started is the home composting website, www.homecomposting.org.uk.

- Refilling containers, there are now many local stores that sell refills of everything from household cleaners to real ale. This is a great way to cut down on your packaging demands. Also, children's packed lunches often contain disposable juice cartons which we simply throw away. Why not use a refillable bottle? Perhaps create a healthy homemade fruit smoothie!

1   Robert and Brenda Vale. (2009) 'Time to Eat the Dog? A guide to sustainable living'. Thames and Hudson
2   Elliot Coleman, (1999) 'The Four Season Harvest'. Chelsea Green

- Rechargeable batteries, many batteries contain harmful toxins and are left to decompose in landfill, although there are now nationwide schemes which allow for the safe disposal of disposable batteries. However, many batteries, like those on our phone or MP3 player are already rechargeable, so why not make the leap for the other batteries we use and buy rechargeable replacements?

- Buy second hand, every time we buy a second hand item, be it an item of clothing, a bike, CD, a piece of furniture or a hi-fi, we reduce the demand for newly manufactured goods and thus we have reduced the potential waste associated with that item and reduced the GHGs associated with brand new products. Moreover, buying second hand can offer up some amazing deals, unexpected finds, and develop a more creative approach to purchasing.

- Resourceful thinking. Think about your waste as a potential resource for someone else. Sell your unwanted things via eBay. Or join a Freecycle Network. Here in Sussex we have a thriving Freegle Network via Yahoo.[1] Here your unwanted items are offered for free and given a last minute reprieve from landfill. Many items that you thought were no good to anyone might just find an appreciative benefactor.

- Reduce unwanted mail, reduce the reliance on paper billing and change your bills to a secure online version only. You could also register with the free Mailing Preference Service (MPS) which helps reduce unwanted direct mail by up to ninety five per cent.

Painting a depressing picture about waste in the UK is well

---

1   Freegle, http://www.freegle.org.uk/

trodden, easy ground to cover, but, as we have seen from the innovative ways we can reduce or reuse our waste as highlighted in this section, things are improving. Our awareness is growing as is our willingness to do something about it.

Recycling rates are no different; all over the UK recycling has increased year on year, and in the south east we have improved from eighteen per cent recycled or composted in 2001 to the thirty nine per cent we achieved in 2009.[1]

It is very difficult to give an accurate overview of recycling in Sussex, as it is everywhere in the UK, because of the different services each borough council deliver. For example, at the moment, residents in Eastbourne can place all of the things residents in Brighton can in curbside recycling boxes with the addition of textiles and shoes. Brighton and Hove residents have to find other ways to recycle these items. This means a trip to a charity shop or one of the local tips.

Local tips are increasingly where we need to look to for the safe disposal of much of our waste especially waste that is classified

1   Crown Copyright: Defra, Municipal Waste Statistics, November 2009: http://www. defra.gov.uk/evidence/statistics/environment/wastats/index.htm

as hazardous. Common hazardous waste from households includes such things as car batteries, paint, asbestos, oils, and pesticides. Local tips and recycling centres are increasingly providing solutions for these types of waste. For example, the WEEE (Waste Electrical and Electronic Equipment) initiative helps reduce electronic materials from finding their way to landfill where toxic chemicals, metals, plastics, and glues will be released causing environmental and health problems. A list of recycling centres near you can be found either through your local borough council's web site or the government site, Act on CO2.[1]

In the years since the EU published its Landfill Directive in 1999 we've seen a great improvement in recycling rates and a reduction in the total amount of waste we produce. We as a nation and as a county are more aware of the issues and much more willing to take responsibility for the waste we create, but we still have a great deal to do in order to achieve truly sustainable waste habits. When it comes to sustainability, and I mean truly sustainable patterns of living that do not adversely affect the environment now or in the future, we might want to give a last word to David MacKay. In his book, 'Without Hot Air',[2] he debunks many myths. One of my favourite is the myth peddled out that 'every little helps', to which he retorts a more realistic manta being, 'if everyone does a little, we'll only achieve a little'. And this is not meant to be a negative statement, not in my view anyway. It is a wakeup call. We get green-washed everyday into thinking that we buy our way out of climate change or offset our guilt in some way or another. When it comes to our waste we should be doing everything we can to reduce our waste to as little as possible, and what is left over is able to decompose usefully.

---

1   Act on CO2: http://actonco2.direct.gov.uk/actonco2/home/what-you-can-do/recycle.html
2   David MacKay, (2008), 'Sustainable Energy – without the hot air,' Cambridge. Also on-line: http://www.withouthotair.com

Continuing to think outside of the recyling box, I question; how many of you reuse or recycle wood? To be honest with you I have never even considered how to recycle wood. However, as Mid Sussex Wood Recycling explain, wood is an easily recyclable resource which often ends up unnecessarily in the land fill site.

Wood recycling by David Treadwell.

Wood is an organic material with many uses, primarily as a construction material for making houses, tools, furniture, packaging and paper. It has also been used as fuel since man discovered fire.

Wood has been an important material for the construction of homes since man began making shelters and even today new domestic housing is still constructed using timber frames. Even in buildings made of other materials, timber is still used in roof supports, interior doors and flooring. Wooden shuttering is used to form the mould into which concrete is poured and wooden scaffold planks are still the preferred option.

Wood has also been the primary material for the construction of furniture, from beds to tables, from Chippendale to Ikea.

In industry, wood has been an important material for packaging goods in order to protect them during transportation and storage.

The recycling of wood comes into its own when the primary use or life of the product is finished. In 2007 the wood waste arising from things including industry, construction and demolition was estimated to amount to more than four and a half million tonnes; it is interesting to note that a lot of this is created by the South East, this is partly due to its high population density.[1]

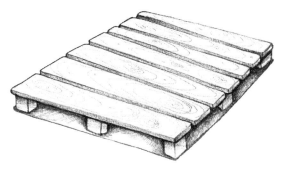

On a worldwide scale, it is estimated that 1.5 billion pallets are produced on a worldwide scale each year.[2] Logistic (freight) companies buy a large number of pallets per year, unfortunately an increasing amount of these are destined for single-use. Some companies' pool pallets for distribution around the UK, the most notable of these are CHEP which use distinctive blue pallets. These are recovered by CHEP when they deliver their next consignment and this ensures as many pallets as possible are kept in their circle of contracts. Any broken pallets are repaired and then put back in circulation. Single use pallets are exactly that. The cost of them is included in the freight

1   Copyright WRAP 2009 http://www.wrap.org.uk/downloads/Wood_waste_mar
         ket_in_the_UK.ec042861.7547.pdf
2   Copyright Timcon: http://www.timcon.org/Publications/FactSheets/Download/
         Fact%20Sheet%20-%20Pallets.pdf

charge and the customer is left with the pallet to dispose of. There are two disposal routes for wood waste, landfill and re-use or recycle.

The Mid Sussex Wood Recycling Project does not consider landfill to be an option for the disposal of such a versatile and reusable material. In Germany, sending wood waste to landfill has been prohibited since 2003 and in my opinion this is a policy change that the UK Government would do well to implement.

Let us look at the reuse and recycle options available:

A high proportion of the wood waste that is recycled - this includes clean packaging wood waste - is used by wood panel manufacturers to create OSB and chipboard sheets. This reduces the need for virgin timber to be used in creating these products and thus reduces the continued pressure on native woodlands to be converted to cultivated plantations.

The other mainstream outlets for clean wood waste are animal bedding, fuel and compost material.

To produce compost material for agricultural and horticultural use the wood waste is shredded and mixed with the green waste collected at civic amenity sites. It is composted down, using a simple windrow process, into reusable products such as soil conditioner, mulch and topsoil. For agriculture the use of this type of compost material can bring savings of almost 200 pounds per hectare, when compared with using chemical fertiliser, and has the added benefit of only using natural ingredients.

Clean packaging waste can also be processed into wood pellets for biomass boilers. The wood collected at civic amenity sites ranges from DIY off-cuts to items of furniture and is either sent for energy generation, where such facilities exist, or, to a lesser extent, to wood panel manufacturers.

Individuals can also utilise waste timber, albeit on a smaller scale, both in the home and garden.

Home:

If you buy real wood furniture you will save yourself the headache of disposing of laminated and chipboard furniture later on. Solid wood furniture can always be revitalised by cleaning and applying Danish oil (or similar). If unwanted, it can be sold, or donated to one of the many charity shops or re-homing organisations for example, Furnihelp, to give it an extended life.

Real wood furniture can also be adapted to create a new piece of furniture. Table tops can be replaced or the legs of a table can be shortened to create a coffee table.

If you have a period home with original doors and are looking to replace them, there will always be somebody interested in taking them from you, either to reinstate original features in their own home or just to have solid well-made doors in their home.

Recycled wood can be used to make new furniture that already has that worn-in look. Old floor joists can be used to create bed frames and old scaffold boards can be used to create bookcases.

Floorboards that have been replaced can be used to make unique picture or mirror frames. They can also be used in a frame to create window shutters.

Garden:

Old planks of timber or scaffold boards can be used to create raised beds for plants and vegetables. Using raised beds in the garden or allotment saves you the effort of having to dig over the soil, especially if it is has clay in it or it is chalky.

Sturdy wooden boxes can be utilised as tree planters with the minimum of preparation.

Pallets and pallet tops can be used to create compost bins in gardens or allotments.

Long plasterboard pallets can be utilised to create a living wall, which is a great way of elevating your garden or hiding the dustbin or compost area.

If you are having a tree felled in your garden you can stack the small logs to create a home for beneficial wildlife alongside your flower and vegetable beds or use longer length logs to edge your beds to create the same environment. Long branches can be used to create a rustic ladder to decorate your garden area.

Garden sheds can be repaired using discarded plywood panels or doors. This is a cheaper option than even the cheapest replacement shed and will be much more durable.

Sawdust is a waste product of joinery companies and is ideal as a mulch for allotments and more environmentally friendly than using carpets or plastic liners as ground cover, it is cheaper too as many joinery companies will give this away in order to save on their disposal costs. It can be used in the garden as a substitute for ornamental bark chippings on pathways and, being denser, is more effective as a weed suppressant. For the adventurous amongst you, sawdust can also be used for the smoking of meat and fish in your DIY smoker at home.

Short lengths of clean timber can be used to build bird boxes for your garden. There are a number of simple and innovative designs to be found on the internet which can be built with simple hand tools and a collection of screws.

Another way to dispose of short lengths of clean timber is to cut them up for your kindling and firewood or donate them to a neighbour who has a real fire or woodstove. You may even be invited in to share the warmth and enjoy a cup of tea.

With thanks to:

David Akroyd. Finding a balance between modern living, business profit and maintaining sustainable practices is a passion for David, not to mention a challenge. He is currently helping his current employers, Whites Bar and Kitchen, battle with a nationwide waste contractor who seem unable even to provide a glass recycling bin.

David Treadwell is the Director of Mid Sussex Wood Recycling Project. Formed in 2007 to rescue, re-use and recycle some of the thousands of tonnes of wood going to landfill locally by collecting wood waste from local businesses. We are a Social Enterprise; a not-for-profit environmental group and financially self-supporting. We offer placements and training to young people or those seeking employment and we encourage volunteers interested in the project and its aims to get involved.

Section 6) Children and the Environment

I believe it is important to educate children and young people to encourage them to be more environmentally aware. Children are the next generation; for all the damage we have done to the planet it is up to the next generations of young people to make sure that history does not repeat itself and that in the future we all take steps to reduce our environmental impact. This section will demonstrate how parents and their children can work together to reduce their family's carbon footprint. How adults can educate the next generation, the most important generation in my opinion, with regards to climate change. Future generations need to understand the implications of climate change from a young age and get into positive, environmentally friendly habits early on.

It is important that children are able to incorporate environmentally friendly activities and attitudes into their daily lives. Philip Hunton explains how you can be more green as a family and Natalie Skinner from Growing up Green children's nursery in Brighton demonstrates the nursery's environmentally friendly ethos with some suggestions as to how you can encourage your children to live a more eco friendly life. Working to combat climate change not only has a positive effect on the environment; it can save your family money and be fun for children too.

There are chapters throughout this book offering you tips and advice as to how you can alter your lifestyle inside the house, outside in the garden and how you can reduce, reuse or recycle your waste. But how can we present this ethos to our children and involve them in our bid to save the planet? We need to make this information accessible to the younger generations, after all, the future, our planet, is ultimately in their hands.

Top tips for green families by Philip Hunton.

For many families being green is often considered as an expensive luxury. Buying organic food and finding time to sort out the recycling can become low on the 'to do' list especially for those on a budget.

However it needn't be a chore, being green can actually save money, improve health and help reduce damage to the planet. Adopting a greener lifestyle can be a rewarding process. Taking pleasure from fresh, locally sourced food, cycling instead of taking the car and lowering utility bills are just a few examples of how being green lessens environmental damage, increases wellbeing and makes good financial sense. Involving your children and explaining why you are making changes inspires and empowers them to protect the environment.

Top Tip! Food for thought.
Understanding and teaching children about food miles, seasonal food and nutrition is essential to understanding our carbon footprint and promoting health and wellbeing. Think about how much food you throw away each day, consider that wastage over a year. Work with your children to plan your family's meals, prepare only what you think will be eaten, you can always prepare more.

Top Tip! Reusing.
Instead of throwing away old toys and clothes, take them to a

charity shop, car boot sale or jumble sale so that someone else can make use of them. Have fun with your children sorting through old clothes and toys and discuss how they can be reused by other children via donating to charity shops. Or have a table top sale with your child where they can see for themselves how their old things can be reused and make some pocket money from it at the same time!

Top Tip! In the kitchen.
Small changes in the kitchen and utility room can add up to big savings in the home. Boiling water on a hob uses large amounts of energy; use the correct size pan and hob. When cooking with your children teach them that boiling water in a kettle before transfering it onto the hob, is more efficient than bringing water to the boil on the hob. Always use a lid on the pan when water is simmering; this saves energy. Using a steamer on top of a pan used for boiling is another way to save and maximise energy on the hob. Practice good habits like these with your children when they are young to ensure they maintain them in the future.

Growing up green by Natalie Skinner.

Babies.

Nappies can take up to 500 years to decompose in a landfill site and a child of two years will have got through on average 4700 nappies. With 708,711 live births recorded in Britain in 2008,[1] that's a lot of nappies! However, there is no need to panic as there are lots of environmentally friendly alternatives available to help our children grow up green!

At Growing up Green for example, we use reusable cotton nappies. These can be washed at sixty degrees, which will effectively sterilise them, or they can be picked up by a laundry service. There are suppliers around Brighton and Hove and there are a number of websites that sell and can advise you about the use of washable nappies.

Alternatively there are environmentally friendly disposable nappies that are available, for example, Moltex Oko nappies. These are chlorine-free, have no unnecessary chemicals and are 100 per cent biodegradable. In fact they are fully compostable within eight weeks so there is no need for them to be sent to the landfill at all.

1   Crown Copyright http://www.statistics.gov.uk/cci/nugget.asp?id=369

Children and food.

Getting children involved in growing food is a really good way of getting them to eat it. Children are fascinated by watching food grow and being a part of helping to make it happen. Encourage them to be involved every step of the way: planting, watering, harvesting and finally, eating. You will be amazed at how excited they get. With younger children especially, it's nice for them to see the fruit or vegetables growing. Choose crops like tomatoes or runner beans. These also grow fairly quickly.

Older children love to have an area they can call their own. Give them a small veggie patch. This not only teaches them about where their food comes from but also teaches them to be responsible and gives them pride in their achievements. You do not need lots of space or even a garden; you can grow lots of different crops inside or in window boxes or containers on a balcony.

Recycling.

At Growing up Green we encourage children to recycle. It is easy and we find most children will recycle automatically by the age of four. At home, make sure that your recycling boxes are at a level that your child can reach and labelled in a way that ensures that they will be able to understand what each box is for. You can encourage your children to recycle by making it fun and through explaining why we should recycle. There are a number of good children's books that you could try. For example: 'Dinosaurs and All That Rubbish' by Michael Foreman and 'The Adventures of a Plastic Bottle' from the Little Green Books series.

Recycling activity for Children by Philip Hunton.

Paper bead making

Here is a simple way to for you and your children to reduce, reuse and recycle and have fun at the same time.

Recycling paper into beads is inexpensive and creative way to recycle.

You will need:

Thin paper
Wood glue or craft glue
Old cardboard
Knitting needle or wood dowel
String

How to make the paper beads.

Work over a piece of paper or piece of old newspaper to avoid making a mess. Use junk mail or glossy magazines to make the beads, as these are colourful.

1. Cut out triangle shapes from your paper. The taller and thinner you make them, the chunkier they will be in the middle.

2. Place your triangle shaped paper on a flat surface; place the knitting needle or wooden dowel along the bottom wide end of the triangle.

3. Roll the wide end of the triangle in on its self around the knitting needle, once it has made a tight tube around the knitting needle glue the paper so that it holds. Then place glue along the remaining part of the triangular paper, which is facing up towards you.

4. Carry on rolling the paper around its self and the knitting needle so that it sticks to itself tightly.

5. Continue this technique with different coloured and sized triangles in order to make a combination of beads for your bracelet or necklace.

Reusing activity for children by Philip Hunton

Reusing a juice carton to make a windowsill salad box

You will need:

Washed out drinks carton
Pen or pencil
Scissors
Gravel
Compost
Seeds

Reusing food and drink packing is a great way to make a statement about the amount of waste we produce. Use a juice carton as a container for planting some salads or rocket.

How to make the salad box.

1. Simply lay the carton onto one side and push a biro into one corner; this gives you a starting point. Cut out one of the large sides of the carton. Use safety scissors and ask an adult to help you.

2. Using your biro, punch six holes on the opposite side of the carton and put some gravel inside the bottom of the carton for drainage. The shape of the carton is perfect to be placed on a sunny window ledge.

3. Fill the carton with compost and plant seeds according to instruction.

4. Remember when growing salads and rocket start planting more when the first salad leaves appear this will ensure that you will have fresh salad for much of the growing season.

Use appropriate caution with scissors, glue, and craft knives.

With thanks to:

Natalie Skinner and Growing Up Green Day Nursery.
Natalie Skinner is a nursery nurse at Growing Up Green Children's Nursery. For more information about the nursery see http://www.growingupgreen.co.uk, telephone: 01273 551333 or email: enquiries@growingupgreen.co.uk

Philip Hunton and Green Up Your Act Education. Green Up Your Act educates children in the meaning of sustainability through interactive workshops using a balance of discussion, practical activities and out of class learning. The project's core objective is to enable children to become aware of their own carbon footprint. This is taught by focusing on subjects such as food, recycling, energy production, biodiversity and pollution. We are hopeful that all the children come away from their experience inspired about their involvement with the environment and empowered that they can make a difference.

Green up your act is now offering green tutoring at home in the form of increasing your gardens biodiversity lowering your electricity bills and green craft workshops at kids eco parties.
Call Philip Hunton for more information: 07739318569

117

SECTION 7) FOOD AND DRINK

Why eat local? By Harvest Brighton and Hove.

Food is such an important part of our lives, and not just because we need to eat to survive! So much is connected to the food we eat, much more so than many of us may realise.

The impacts of our current food system (the technical term for how food gets from the farm to your fork) on the world around us are enormous. The way that the majority of our food is grown and transported is hugely resource-intensive (especially on water and oil), and is often harmful to the environment. Plus, many farmers both here in the UK, and overseas, don't receive a fair price for their produce due to competing pressures to keep prices low. And supermarkets, convenient though they may be, mean that many of us have lost the connection with where food really comes from.

However, there are so many ways we can all make a difference. Consuming more food and drink produced in your local area supports farmers and local businesses and helps them to flourish. Shopping at farmers' markets and using vegetable box schemes means you buy directly from the farmer and producer, ensuring they get a fair price for their produce. Plus, you get the added bonus of meeting the people involved in growing your courgettes, baking your bread and making your cheese. Eating local food also helps to reduce the negative affects our food systems have on the environment because the food doesn't have to travel so far before we eat it. When buying food and drink that can't be produced locally (like bananas, coffee, tea and sugar), look out for the fair trade logo so you know that the grower has received a fair price for their produce.

Because we're so used to eating fruit and veg all year round, we've lost touch with what's in season when. Eating local food means we can rediscover seasonality. Sure it means you can't eat fresh tomatoes or strawberries in December, but you look forward to them all the more when summer rolls around and they definitely taste better for it!

Whether you're eating out or cooking at home, take a moment to think about how your food was grown and where it has come from. If you want to find out more you can go to the Harvest website where you can read about the many shops, farmers' markets and box schemes in Brighton and Hove, to ensure you are eating food that supports the producer and the environment.

Food miles and climate change.

From the methane produced by the cows and paddy fields to driving your car to the supermarket, the food system – growing crops, raising, processing, packaging food, transporting food, eating food and throwing away food waste – makes significant contributions to our green house gas emissions. This subsequently contributes to climate change and will increasingly impact on what, how and where we grow food.

You may have heard of the term 'food miles', this is used to denote how far food travels from the farm to the plate. This includes the journey from farm to processor, then from processor to retailer, from retailer to consumer and finally the journey home from the shop to the plate. It includes travel within the UK as well as between countries.

Transporting food long distances uses a lot of fuel, whether the food travels by lorry, plane or boat. However some people have criticised the term 'food miles' because it doesn't include the impact of how the food is produced, packaged, stored and cooked, or even how you get to the shop to buy it – all of which can have a negative impact on the environment.

Despite its limitations, 'food miles' can still be a useful way of thinking about the environmental impact of our food. No matter what term you use, the key idea is to reduce carbon dioxide emissions and therefore global warming. There are lots of things you can do; the choices you make when you go shopping can make a difference…

Why buy local food? 'It's thousands of miles fresher'.
Ten good reasons to buy local food.

1. To support your local economy; buying locally produced food supports local businesses and creates employment opportunities.
2. To reduce food miles; when you buy locally produced food, it travels a much shorter distance to reach your plate, and therefore helps the environment by producing fewer greenhouse gas emissions.
3. It's just so fresh; when you buy local food, either from a shop or directly from the farmer or producer, chances are you're getting the freshest possible food.

4. To reduce waste and packaging; buying local food straight from the farmer helps both you and them reduce food and packaging waste.

5. You know where your food comes from; buying local food, especially directly from the farmer, gives the customer the chance to learn about how the food was grown and know where it comes from.

6. It's healthier; locally grown and produced food is fresher - you're likely to get it within days of it being picked. The fresher the food the more nutrients it retains.

7. To support local farmers; whether you buy at a farmers' market, through a veg box scheme, or at the farm, your support helps farmers stay in business and ensures farming skills and traditions stay alive and flourish.

8. Eat with the seasons; buying food produced locally means that you are eating seasonal foods, the way that nature intended.

9. Lots of choice; local farmers often grow varieties of foods you won't find in supermarkets. Buying local gives you the chance to try new things and keeps our food system diverse and exciting!

10. Quality; buying local food helps ensure you'll be eating top quality, fresh and delicious food!

Things you can do to reduce the environmental impact of your food:

- shop locally, use farmers' markets, vegetable box schemes and small local independent retailers. Alternatively shop online.
- Try getting together with friends to set up a food buying co-operative; buying produce in bulk costs less and uses less packaging.
- Try walking, cycling or taking the bus to do your shopping.
- If you have to drive, try shopping once a week rather than lots of small trips throughout the week.
- Eat lower on the food chain as fruit and vegetable production requires far less energy than meat production.
- If you do eat meat, buy free-range, organically raised meat and poultry products. These should have been raised humanely and on untreated feeds.
- Eating organically grown local fruits and vegetables doesn't just reduce the amount of pesticides getting released into the environment; it's also healthier for you, the farmers and the food handlers.
- Eat local fruits and vegetables which are fresher and less likely to be waxed.
- Buy vegetables loose not vegetables that have been packaged.
- Try growing your own vegetables, fruits and herbs without using pesticides.
- Look more closely at country-of-origin labels on food products and choose your purchases accordingly.
- Ask politely (but firmly) where food comes from when shopping and even when eating out.
- Eat foods that are in season in the UK.
- Use farm shops or pick-your-own farms.
- Look for local food producers on the internet.

As we have highlighted, purchasing locally produced food is a great way to reduce our impact on the environment as well as ensuring we consume fresh and healthy food. Harvest Brighton and Hove have presented a solid case for consumers to make an effort to shop locally.

But remember, it is important to distinguish between simply locally produced food and food that is marketed as organic. As Marian Harding of Court Lodge Organics explains, to be certified as an organic producer, farmers have to abide by strict rules and regulations.

Organic farming by Marian Harding.

Organic farming is all about:

- Trying to farm with nature not against it.
- Not having pesticides, herbicides or insecticides on the farm.
- Aiming to be sustainable, avoiding external inputs where possible.
- Producing healthy food to be proud of.
- Having healthy livestock that have a good life and are respected.
- Making a difference to wildlife.
- Feeling very lucky to live on an organic farm!

My thoughts about organic…

Organic food is without a doubt better for the planet. Chemical sprays have done so much harm to wildlife, and their manufacture uses a lot of resources. By avoiding non-organic food, you can avoid being part of that system. It is better to be safe rather than sorry!

Organic food avoids pesticides and all controversial additives including aspartame, tartrazine, MSG and hydrogenated fats. Personally I don't think that our bodies are meant to take in these things and think it's just best to avoid them altogether.

Organic food is tasty food! Organic food is naturally produced and often more nutritious and tasty than more intensively reared food. This may be down to how it's produced. For example, cows fed on a high clover diet produce milk with a higher omega 3 fatty acid content and food grown with artificial fertiliser often produces more watery vegetables than slower growing organic veggies.

Alternatively it could be because most organic foods are not highly processed. Highly processed foods such as some ready meals are often bulked out with starchy ingredients and are often rather short on vitamin and nutritional content.

We are certified!

From a practical point of view, to call your produce organic, you must obviously be able to prove that you're not cheating in any way. This is done by annual inspections by various organisations that are licensed to 'certify' farmers as bona-fide organic producers. One such organisation is the soil association;[1] you can look up the standards online.

---

1   http://www.soilassociation.org/

To get certified you need precise records of all your inputs (which must themselves be certified organic) and outputs. All your activities are monitored and inspections rigorously adhered to agreed EU standards. This needs to be done for at least two years (the conversion period) before any produce from that land counts as organic.

Occasionally people try to call their produce organic when they don't use chemicals themselves but are unsure about some other aspects of their production. This isn't correct as everything in the food chain must be organic. For example, organic chickens must only be fed with organically produced feed which is made from organic oats that must be grown on organically certified land using organically produced seed and so on. You must meet specific standards with regards to animal welfare, waste management, nutrient management and wildlife protection and you must be able to prove it. There are separate standards for all manner of things, from aquaculture to woodland and a whole host of things in between.

Thinking about the whole food chain is important. Before we became fully organic, we already cared for our land and cattle in much the same way as we do now but the main change for us has been in the sourcing of cattle feed. Non-organic farms can source feed from wherever it's most economic, whereas all feed for organic animals must be certified organic, so the feed is grown on an organic crop rotation, which tends to have great benefits for wildlife and is guaranteed GM free.

Obviously the dairy cows all graze on grass in the summer months, but in the winter when there's no grass growth, they have to be fed on feed saved from the plentiful months. On our farm this feed is made from a variety of crops which are rotated around the farm to maintain fertility. We use grass and red clover to provide protein in the feed and fix nitrogen from the atmosphere, wheat to provide energy and starch, and then a mixed 'whole crop' such as oats and peas, planted in spring after the wheat.

The rotation means that we do perfectly well without any chemical inputs whatsoever, avoid build-up of weeds and pests, and provide a variety of wildlife habitats within the farm. Our young cattle are fed on hay made on the outlying pastures but, like many dairy farmers, we don't have enough suitable land to grow all the feed we need, so some 'concentrated' feed is bought in from outside. This has to come from other organic farms, who will also be farming without chemicals, so even if, like us, you can't grow all the feed necessary yourself, you can be sure it comes from other farms that are free of chemicals.

Some facts about organic food.

Producing organic food means that no routine antibiotic treatments can be used for animals. Prevention rather than cure is the aim and organic livestock farmers are encouraged to use other methods of disease control, using herbal and homeopathic remedies, and only using antibiotics for animals that are sick.

126

Organically reared animals must have a healthy diet and ample space. The annual inspections rigorously scrutinise the use of animal medicines and you can lose your organic certification if you get it wrong. Animal welfare is paramount and it's not acceptable to withhold medicine from an animal that is suffering. There are also strict controls to make sure the milk or meat from that animal isn't sold as organic until an appropriate 'antibiotic free' period has elapsed.

Organic food is always dirty. All vegetables grown in the ground will have some soil and dirt on them; this is normal and should not put you off eating the food. Large scale producers can justify the expense of equipment to wash it off. However it won't keep so well after washing, and often crops are washed in chemicals so you need to wash them again to wash off the chemicals.

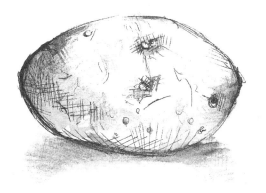

Organic food is sometimes more expensive. This is because organic food is less intensively produced therefore yields are often lower, herds and flocks tend to be smaller and more carefully managed, so labour costs per unit are usually higher. The difference can often be made up by choosing what's in season and buying simple rather than processed and packaged food, and cheaper cuts of meat which are equally tasty and nutritious.

Cooking one large family meal from basic ingredients, rather than using ready meals, is healthy and cheaper, I often make double quantities and freeze some for later, then I have a home-made ready meal for another day!

Organic milk is a bit more expensive than non-organic, but for a family using a pint a day, the difference would be less than one pound a week. Organic milk is also a great source of calcium, vitamins, essential fatty acids and anti-oxidants.

Adding value.

Even with a small price premium above non-organic milk, we found that by selling our milk wholesale we weren't really covering our costs adequately. Therefore back in 2001 we decided to try to add value to it. Some years earlier we did an exchange trip with some Dutch dairy farmers, under a scheme called 'Eurolink', and spent an interesting time in Holland. There we found that the shops stocked a huge range of yoghurt and flavoured milk drinks, which families would always have on the breakfast table. Some of these were delicious and very healthy, and since nobody else in Sussex was making them, we decided to have a go.

I went on a course at Reaseheath College in Cheshire and learnt to make yoghurt. We fitted out a shed at the back of the milking parlour, with advice from our local environmental health officer, and we bought some second hand equipment and then we got started. It was a steep learning curve, inevitably involving lots of red tape, more organic certification and many hours and tastings, but we now have a range of tasty yoghurt drinks.

Our yoghurt drinks are still made on a very small scale and, unlike factory made yoghurt, the milk goes from udder to 'yoghurt in a bottle' in under twenty four hours, having travelled only about twenty metres! We don't 'process' the milk by standardisation or homogenisation, we simply pasteurise it by heating and adding some 'friendly bacteria', so ours is a really natural yoghurt drink.

Several local people come and help stick labels on and fill the bottles by hand, and we sell them through local shops, some Waitrose stores and farmers' markets in London, and several box schemes. Most people think they are delicious!

Life of a cow on our organic farm.

Of course it is cyclical, so where to start, the cow or the calf? Let's start with our typical cow. She's a British Friesian, black and white, a fairly dumpy shape compared with the higher yielding Holstein. This comparison is rather like comparing a highland pony with a racehorse. The former is steady, tough and long lived; the latter is fast, delicate and burns out after a few years of hard work.

The cow is milked twice a day in a 'milking parlour', at five am and three pm, for ten months of the year. Over that time she will probably give us 5000 - 6000 litres of milk, compared to a non-organic Holstein which might give 10,000 litres. In winter she lives in a strawed barn, in summer she grazes on grass meadows, with the rest of the herd. She's 'served' by artificial insemination (AI) when she comes into season. Naturally, no hormone treatments to artificially interfere with breeding are allowed, and if success-fully impregnated she will have a calf nine months later. A cow that hasn't 'held' to the AI will eventually get a chance to have 'the real thing' with our Aberdeen Angus bull, and produce a 'beef cross' calf to be reared for meat or breeding more beef cows.

A couple of months before she's due to calve, she will be 'dried off'. This means cutting down on her food and encouraging her milk to stop flowing, and she will have her 'summer holi-day'. Many of our cows spend their summer holiday on the Sus-sex Wildlife Trust's Pevensey Marsh reserve, which is rented to us. The cows help to maintain the wet grassland that is so good for wetland birds and invertebrates. Grazing livestock is the only way of looking after this sort of habitat – so when you buy organic dairy products, and beef and lamb, you are helping to look after the wildlife that thrives on this rich grassland.

When she's ready to calve, the cow will be brought back to a field near the farm buildings, or into a barn if its winter, so we're on hand if she has any trouble calving. When the calf arrives it stays with the cow for a couple of days, to suckle and get the 'first milk' or colostrum, which contains vital antibodies, essential for its health. It will then be taken away and kept in a pen with other calves, and fed on milk from the milking parlour. This may seem a bit unkind, but we find that the longer the calves are left with their mother, the more upset cow and calf are when they are sep-arated.

Dairy cows are obviously bred to produce much more milk than one calf needs, in order to provide us with surplus for ourselves, and we find that the cow settles very quickly when she gets into the milking parlour, where she gets fed. The calves are reared in groups of five on organic milk from artificial teats, which they take to very easily. On non-organic dairy farms, calves are often reared on 'milk replacer', a powder that may contain vegetable fat and other ingredients as well as dried milk, and is mixed with water to a milky consistency. Organic dairy calves must be fed on organic milk for at least twelve weeks, before being weaned onto organic feed, whereas non-organic calves may be weaned earlier, which saves labour and money.

What happens to the calves? Friesian dairy calves (heifers) are reared on the farm to join the dairy herd in due course. Friesian male calves are sold to other local farmers to rear for beef, and the Aberdeen Angus cross calves are reared on the farm until about eighteen months old, helping to maintain the wet grassland on our farm and the nature reserve next door, when they are sold to a specialist organic beef farmer to be fattened as quality organic beef.

After two or three years the Friesian heifers will be ready to calve themselves and join the herd, and the cycle begins again!

I remember many years ago when I was at college, I was completing a lecture on a horticulture course. The lecturer arrived with two cabbages, a non organic one bought from a supermarket, and one from his own garden, grown without chemicals. He parted the leaves on his cabbage and removed a number of slugs and caterpillars, to the disgust of the class. He placed the creatures among the leaves of the supermarket cabbage, and proceeded to deliver his lecture (about which nobody could remember very much!).

At the end of the lecture he parted the leaves of the supermarket cabbage and removed the slugs and caterpillars...they had all died! Which cabbage would you prefer to eat?

One of the best opportunities for sourcing locally produced food is at a farmer's market. The idea of visiting a farmer's market for the first time may seem a little daunting compared to the organised aisles of a supermarket, but it does not need to be. Hilary Knight, Coordinator of a Taste of Sussex food group, offers us an expert's guide to shopping at a farmer's market.

Farmers' markets, with their emphasis on fresh, seasonal produce and their hands-on approach to shopping, are a magnet for food-lovers. Factor in the shoppers' chances to chat to the growers and possibly pick up a recipe from fellow food-lovers, and you have a formula for food-shopping success.

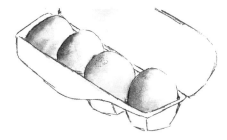

Shopping at a farmer's market by Hilary Knight.

Shopping at your local farmer's market brings a host of environmental, social and economic benefits. Firstly, it reduces your number of 'food miles' as all of the products will have been produced in the local area. Secondly, it gives you an opportunity to talk to producers and find out more about the products you are buying. Thirdly, the range of products available is often wider than at a supermarket. Products sold at supermarkets have to be robust enough for mass sale and transportation, so more unusual vegetables and local delicacies will not be stocked. Markets provide an invaluable forum for specialist growers, and will often give them a bigger profit margin than selling through a wholesaler.

As with all food shopping, there are some specific points to consider:

1. write a list...
    Consider how much food you waste each week? Most of us throw away vast amounts of perfectly edible food because we over cater.

    Modern food shopping is based around one large weekly shop. Although an efficient use of time, it is not the ideal way to buy food. It means that you have to ripen products at home, freeze or store them. Doing smaller, regular shops and buying fresh, ripe produce should mean that you save money and reduce waste. Writing a list is one small step towards reconnecting with your ingredients and how much food you actually need.

2. ...but don't stick to it!
    The beauty of a farmer's market is the availability of unusual local or artisan products. Why buy the same things (for example spinach and carrots) every time you go? Ask questions; how do you cook it? Can you taste some? What do you serve with it? Is it free-range? Stall holders often have recipe cards or recomendations you can follow if you are unsure.

3. Find a market that suits you close to home...
    Sussex has sixty regular markets held all over the county on different days. Some have better disabled access than others, some are open longer and they all have a different range of stall holders. Visit several markets local to you in order to find one that best suits your needs www.atasteofsussex.co.uk has up to date lists or you could visit the Sussex Food Finder

at www.sussexfoodfinder.co.uk. The Sussex Food Finder contains a listing of markets, shops and restaurants specialising in local produce and a directory of useful food organisations.

4. ...but also look further afield.
    Remember that local food is not just available at farmer's markets. You can buy local food at supermarkets. A Taste of Sussex is the local food group for the Sussex area. Members use the blue Adonis butterfly logo to highlight the provenance of their products, the butterly lives on the South Downs. This butterfly was chosen to signify Sussex produce as it is a symbol of regeneration. The butterfly was extremely rare but, after concerted local action, its future is more assured. Look out for the blue butterfly when you shop to support your local food and drink producers.

5. Bring cash.
    Smaller vendors may well not have credit card machines. Remembering to bring cash will make the shopping trip run more smoothly.

6. Arrive early.
    If you get there early, you can often find seasonal fruit or vegetables that were harvested within twenty four hours of delivery to the market. You get the best selection and there are fewer people. The stall holders are less busy and will have more time to chat.

7. Eat food that is in season at home...
   Seasonal produce is usually cheaper as it is more plentiful, and it is also at its nutritional best. If you are unsure about what is available and when, buy a seasons calendar for your kitchen and check it before you shop.

8. ...and when you are out.
   As the local food movement gathers pace, more and more cafes, restaurants and hotels are putting together local menus. The Sussex Breakfast initiative has been extremely well supported; local businesses can sign up to be accredited 'Sussex Breakfast' providers. Each breakfast must be made from at least sixty per cent of local, seasonal ingredients sourced from Sussex farms using traditional, natural methods with high animal welfare standards.

   To be launched in 2010 is the Sussex Menu, creating a range of brunch, lunch and supper dishes that provide an effective showcase for our local produce. The quality and range of food produced locally is astounding.

Changing your shopping habits does more than increase your choice of ingredients. There is a wealth of long term potential benefits for Sussex. The more local food we eat, the lower our food miles are, reducing pollution and lowering our carbon footprint. From a commercial point of view, initiatives such as the Sussex Menu could prove a valuable new market for local farmers and food producers, resulting in the growth of local distribution chains and associated companies. It would also improve the quality of a visitor's experience, possibly leading to increased spending and repeat stays. 'Gastro-tourism' is a growing market, one which Sussex is well placed to capitalise on.

So, next time you see a farmer's market; stop. Have a look. Try something. You never know, you might like it.

Now that you have bought your food locally it is time to demonstrate how you can create meals using predominantly locally produced ingredients. As we have already mentioned, shopping locally usually means shopping seasonally.

Aimee Cleary from Infinity Foods offers some easy to follow summer recipes that rely strongly on locally produced ingredients.

Starter -Serves 4

Molten goats cheese, sundried tomato, and basil balls served with sugar free caramelised red onion on a bed of summer leaves.

Ingredients:

500g goats cheese
20g sundried tomatoes
20g fresh basil

2 large eggs
50g wholemeal organic flour
100g fresh wholemeal breadcrumbs

1 large red onion
1tbsp lemon juice
1tbsp red wine vinegar
2tbsp agave syrup

Fresh seasonal leaves for example rocket, baby chard, or watercress

Where to find these ingredients...

The goats cheese can be sourced from Sussex High Weald, which is a family run business in Ashdown forest. They use organic milk in their cheeses from animals on the farm and supply both the Infinity shop and cafe with their produce.

The sundried tomatoes used are the Infinity own brand which are organic and ethically sourced for the business. These can be purchased from our shop or ordered through our warehouse.

The salad ingredients are plentiful during the summer months from many local suppliers, such as Lanes organic farm and Seasons; these can also be purchased from our shop.

The recipe uses eggs which we source from Hoads farm, which is Sussex-based and is one of the few remaining traditional farms which supplies both our cafe and shop with delicious free range eggs.

To make the molten goats cheese balls.

Pre soak the sundried tomatoes in hot water for half an hour. Then drain and cool under cold water. Chop into small pieces.

Finely chop the basil

Crumble the goats cheese into a bowl and mix in the basil and tomatoes. Season with sea salt and cracked black pepper.

Form the mixture into small balls. They should each weigh around 25 grams

In a separate bowl mix the eggs together. Don't worry about beating them well, they just need to be combined.

Line up the flour, the eggs and the breadcrumbs next to each other.

Dip the goats cheese balls first into the flour, then into the egg and finally into the breadcrumbs, making sure it has a good roll around in each. They should have a nice coating of breadcrumbs.

When they are all done, gently heat some sunflower oil in a frying pan and place them in it, turning frequently until they are golden brown.

When this is achieved, place them into an oven on 180 degrees for five to ten minutes to ensure the middle is molten.

To serve; stack three or four balls in the middle of a small plate on top of some nice green seasonal leaves (rocket would go especially well) and top with a spoonful of caramelised red onion.

To make the caramelised red onion.

Begin by heating some olive oil or unsalted butter in a pan. For olive oil use 15ml, butter use 20g.

Finely slice one red onion and add to the pan.

Soften for a few minutes.

In a jug mix the lemon juice and red wine vinegar and then pour this, with a pinch of sea salt, onto the onions.

Cook until the onions are soft and then add the agave.

Continue to cook for a further five minutes then transfer into a container and leave to cool.

Main Course - Serves 4 - 6

*Summer risotto of asparagus, slipcote sheeps cheese
and watercress served with crusty bread.*

Ingredients:

*4 shallots finely chopped
4 tbsp olive oil
400g risotto (aborio) rice
60g unsalted butter
2 pints vegetable stock
250g slipcote sheeps cheese
1 bunch of asparagus
250g watercress
sea salt and cracked black pepper.*

Where to find these ingredients...

Asparagus comes into season in the UK in May and June.

The sheeps cheese and butter once again can be bought from Sussex High Weald Dairies and are sold through our shop.

The vegetables can be sourced from various organic local farms and the shops produce department can be relied on for an exciting range.

How to make the risotto:

Snap the asparagus spears, this can be done by bending them until they break, they will naturally snap at the right place and this should be the same for all the spears in the bunch.

Drop the tips into some boiling water for about three minutes, then remove and refresh in cold water and set aside.

Heat the olive oil in a pan and gently fry the shallots in it.

When they have softened, add the risotto rice and fry gently for a few minutes, stirring all the time to make sure the rice doesn't stick to the bottom or burn.

Then add the white wine and continue to stir until the wine is absorbed by the rice.

Make sure it is not cooked at a high temperature. It is time consuming but it is important that everything is absorbed slowly. Remember to keep stirring!

If some stray pieces of rice go up the sides of the pan, brush them back down, if not they shall remain uncooked and you will have crunchy bits in your risotto.

Next slowly add the stock. Do this, bit by bit, allowing every addition to be absorbed before you add the next.

When all the stock has been absorbed try the rice, it should now be soft but still with a little bit of bite to it. If you think it needs a little more cooking, add a bit more stock.

Then remove from the heat and stir in the butter, the asparagus tips and the watercress. Season to taste with sea salt and cracked black pepper. Serve immediately with crusty fresh bread.

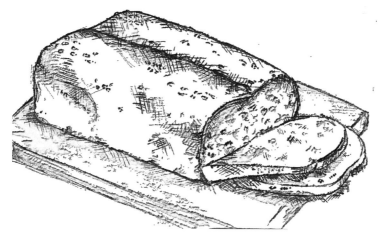

Dessert - Serves 6

Raw chocolate tart with fresh summer berries

Ingredients:

For the base:

60g raw cocoa powder
30g ground almonds
40g agave syrup
30g raw cocoa butter
pinch sea salt

For the filling:

120g raw cocoa powder
150g agave
120g raw cocoa butter
50g chopped dates

Where to find these ingredients...

This tart is made using raw cocoa powder and raw cocoa butter which is supplied to both the cafe and the shop by a local company called Choc Chick.

The ingredients are not local but imported from South America. However we feel it is important to support Choc Chick as they are working with suppliers in South America to produce fair trade and organic produce. They are linked with a worker's co-operative over there, ensuring all workers are treated well and have decent pay as well as producing goods that are environmentally safe. Choc Chick does not yet have organic or fair trade status but this is in the pipe line.

Raw chocolate is become increasingly popular for its health benefits and delicious taste.

How to make the base.

Place the cocoa butter into a bowl and melt over a pan of water.

Combine all ingredients in a food processor and blitz until combined.

Line a cake small cake tin (4 or 5 inches) with grease proof paper and push the base into it, smoothing down with the back of a spoon.

How to make the filling.

Again melt the cocoa butter in a bowl over hot water.
Combine all ingredients in a blend and then pour out onto the crust.

Allow to set in the fridge for one hour and then decorate the top with raw cocoa nibs

Serve with fresh summer berries.

The included recipes, where possible, use locally produced ingredients. Locally produced food does not necessarily equal organic. As Marian Harding has explained, to be organic the producer needs to comply with strict rules and regulations. St Martin's Tea Rooms in Chichester are certified 100 per cent organic. Keith Nelson from the Tea Rooms has provided us with an all year round organic recipe that you can try at home.

Main Course - Serves 2

Salmon Quiche.

Ingredients:

For the filling:

11 eggs: organic free range -
mixed together
500g oat milk: organic
2g pepper: organic
4g paprika: organic
2 stock cubes: dissolved organic
200g onion: finely chopped, organic
4 (20g) crushed garlic: organic
30g olive oil: organic cold pressed virgin
400g smoked salmon: finely chopped, organic
100g raw spinach: chopped, organic
or 250g broccoli: organic
120g mushrooms: finely chopped, organic.

Salmon Quiche.

Ingredients:

For the pastry:

380g flour: wholemeal organic doves
130g olive oil: cold pressed organic virgin
130g cold water

How to make the salmon quiche:

To make the pastry: mix the ingredients together to prepare the pastry.

Mix together the ingredients for the filling and place into raw pastry case then cook.

Cook at 160°C /320°F
For approx 35 mins

With thanks to:

Jess Crocker, Sarah Walters and Ann Baldridge from Harvest Brighton and Hove.

Marian Harding: Marian Harding and her family farm on the edge of Pevensey Marsh, it's a dairy farm and they produce tasty organic yogurt drinks under the 'Court Lodge' label, available in many Sussex independent and farm shops. They won the SE region 'Nature of Farming Award' in 2009 for the most wildlife friendly farm. To see a bit of the farm, its cows and its wildlife, visit: www.courtlodgeorganics.co.uk

Useful sites about organic produce:
Lots of info about the benefits of organic food on the Soil Association website. http://www.soilassociation.org/
Info about organic milk at www.organicmilk.co.uk

Hilary Knight from A taste of Sussex;
http://www.sussexenterprise.co.uk/viewPage.jsp?id=2054334

Aimee Cleary works for Infinity cafe which is part of the Infinity workers co-op. The cafe use only organic food and are hoping to be certified as organic in the near future. They sell their products not just through the cafe but also in the shop and hope that they speak for themselves in showing the benefits of using wherever possible local and organic produce.

Keith Nelson, St Martins tea Rooms. These tea-rooms represent a genuine attempt to recreate in Chichester an almost vanished tradition. In their quiet unassuming Englishness, such establishments were once essential to the life of any town or city. So often they were havens of good taste good simple food and lively conversation. Alas, they have mostly given way to plastic interiors and equally plastic standardised fare. We believe that St Martin's contains all the right ingredients, without artificiality or pretence, but with perhaps a touch of welcome nostalgia.

The terraced house is typical of Chichester's vernacular architecture, with its eighteenth century facade and mediaeval interior. It has been most sensitively restored and furnished relegating modernity to the kitchen where we have achieved exceptional standards of hygiene. We even have a small pretty garden which if not too often suitable for eating 'al fresco' in this climate, at least refreshes the eye. Our food is all truly home-made. We look forward to seeing you

SECTION 8) LEISURE AND LIFESTYLE

Trying to maintain an eco-friendly lifestyle does not have to be boring or expensive. In fact, some of the best hobbies come for free, and make the most of our country's natural resources and surrounding environment.

This section of the book, with a little help from some Sussex locals, will demonstrate how we can have a great day out, or a holiday, making the most of our free time while protecting the local environment. It will also look at our shopping habits and beauty regimes and demonstrate how they do not need to have negative implications for our environment.

A Sunday afternoon stroll by Katie Ramsay

Walking in the countryside; this is a pretty obvious eco friendly activity that we can all partake in. What can be better than spending a day walking along the South Downs? Stretching over one hundred miles (160 kilometres), the South Downs Way follows the age-old winding paths that criss-cross the countryside between Eastbourne to Winchester. I am not suggesting that you walk the whole route (although you could, but perhaps not in one day), but why not spend a morning, an afternoon or even a couple of days exploring the countryside near where you live.

Wherever you live in Sussex I bet you are a mere stones throw away from lush rolling hills and more butterflies and flowers than you can shake your walking stick at. Why not combine a pleasant stroll with lunch in a country pub en route or stop over in a traditional bed and breakfast along the way?

Now to add a hint of controversy to the equation; why not spend your free time exploring the countryside but…wait for it… leave the car at home. Take the Bus for a Walk is an initiative that offers a number of walks that start at one bus stop and finish at another. The initiative hopes that through encouraging us to use public transport to access the South Downs we can stop air and noise pollution in the beautiful countryside that really is just on our doorstep.

There are eighteen 'Bus Walks' available, covering areas from Beachy Head through to Worthing. The walks are all set at varying levels of difficulty and length, so there is something for everyone.

We have included a couple of the more simple walks to get you started, courtesy of the Take the Bus for a Walk campaign, but there are plenty more available online at :
http://www.visitsouthdowns.com.

Beeding

This is just one of the walks on offer from the South Downs Joint Committee. You can easily access this walk from Brighton city centre by hopping on the regular bus route 2A towards Shoreham. You can take the 2A or the number 46 back to Brighton from the finishing point.

The route is approximately four miles long and should take around two hours to complete.

Ordnance Survey Explorer Maps - EX122 - Brighton and Hove

Start point: Dacre Gardens, Shoreham Road. (2A bus route)

End point: Old Shoreham Road (2A bus route) or Holmbush Way (46 bus route), Southwick.

- Head north along the road from the bus stop at Dacre Gardens. On the east side of the road, opposite the car park, take the South Downs Way up to Beeding Hill. Take the bridleway between the bend of the road, heading south east.
- At the end of the bridleway you will reach a T-junction. Turn right and head south towards Southwick Hill.
- Continue on this bridleway through the open access land to Southwick Hill. If you have time why not explore the area and take in the views across the downs and down to the coast?
- The bridleway will take you over the tunnel, and to a fork in the road. Take the right fork and travel down past the dew pond towards North Southwick.
- Upon reaching the houses, follow Upper Kingston Lane down to Old Shoreham Road to catch the 2a Bus. Alternatively turn left at Holmbush Way to pick up the 46 route back towards Brighton.

Seven Sisters:

This is another easily accessible walk. Whether you are coming from the direction of Brighton or Eastbourne this walk is popular and simple to find. Regular bus routes 12, 12A and 13 all pass through this area.

This route is approximately three miles long and should take around one and a half hours to complete.

Ordnance Survey Explorer Maps - EX123 Eastbourne and Beachy Head

Start Point: Chyngton Lane (12, 12A, 13 bus route)

End Point: Exceat Bridge by the Golden Galleon Pub (12, 12A, 13 bus route)

- From the bus stops at Chyngton Lane go up Chyngton Lane and head straight on until the concrete road joins just past Chyngton Farm.
- Go along the concrete road up the hill to South Hill Barn.
- At South Hill Barn car park bear left, go through the barrier and take the middle path.
- Turn right at the cattle grid and down the valley to Hope Gap.
- At Hope Gap turn left at the unfenced cliff edge. From here you will get excellent views of Seven Sisters Cliffs.
- At the Coastguard Cottages go across the track onto the footpath which leads up the valley to Exceat Bridge.

(Please note that all information is correct at the time of going to press. The South Downs was designated as a National Park in March 2010. A fully operational Park Authority will be in place on 1st April 2011.)

For a less stringent stroll, you can take a 'Breeze Bus' from Brighton city centre up to one of three beautiful areas: currently you can take the bus route 77 to Devil's Dyke, the route 78 to Stanmer Park or the route 79 for some spectacular views from Ditchling Beacon. Rather than following a set route you can take any number of footpaths from these locations and take in the spectacular scenery around you. For more information on the Breeze Buses visit www.brighton-hove.gov.uk/breezebuses.

Being beautiful does not mean that you have to spend hundreds of pounds on expensive brand cosmetics which pump lots of chemicals into your skin and whose manufacture potentially damages the environment. Being beautiful can come from making your own beauty therapies from mainly natural ingredients rejuvenating your skin and protecting the environment at the same time.

Environmentally friendly cosmetics by Sophie Adler-Mckean.

Making your own beauty products and cosmetics at home is easy, fun and creative. It is cost effective, as you can usually find the required ingredients at home, and you only need to make a small amount at a time which means little or no wastage. It has positive health benefits as you know exactly what has gone into the product, and you can easily adjust recipes to suit your own needs.

Environmental issues with cosmetics.

There are environmental benefits to making your own cosmetics. Think for a moment, about the materials and energy needed to produce the packaging for just one dose of face mask. (Incidentally, this is the product which I find is the easiest to create at home.) The global cosmetics industry uses a vast amount of packaging which is hardly ever recycled and almost entirely unrecyclable. In some parts of Europe, measures are being taken to introduce recycled glass for use in the packaging of most cosmetic products, but this may not happen for a very long time.

Healthy skin.

One of the main reasons I like to make my own lotions and potions is because I have a knowledge of and respect for the ingredients that I use, and the properties that they contain. I am fascinated by the different ways they can help heal, rejuvenate, calm, energise and balance the body in a gentle and holistic way. (Holistic means treating the body as a whole not just a long list of complaints and symptoms.) All this without needing to spend loads of money, or put my faith into massive corporations who have little concern for my - or anyone else's – actual welfare.

It has been widely reported that the average woman can absorb up to 4lb 6oz of chemicals every year. It has been estimated that if you use ten products a day (shampoo, moisturiser, make up and so on) you could be applying around 175 different chemicals to your face and body on a daily basis.[1] The skin is very porous and the build up of chemicals over years of use can cause damage to the vital organs. If you are interested in finding out more about these chemicals, a useful online tool is at cosmeticsdatabase. com. Here you can type in the name or brand of a product and it will show you a breakdown of the ingredients and how harmful they can be using a points system.

---

1   Copyright British Skin Foundation

Most big cosmetics companies are looking for profit over any-thing else and therefore when designing a new product they will be mainly considering how long it will last, how well it will travel and how to make it smell nice in the cheapest way possible. So after heavy chemical preservatives and potentially toxic artificial fragrances have been added, the properties claimed by the prod-uct are going to have little effect, if any at all.

This doesn't mean that all natural products you make or buy will only last a few days. The ones that are the most complicated to make (for example, hand creams, lip balms and moisturisers) can last anywhere from six months to two years. It all depends on the water content and whether the ingredients you use happen to contain natural preservatives and antioxidants such as grape seed oil, tea tree, lemon and rosemary.

Oil and butter (cocoa butter, shea butter) based products will last much longer than water and milk based ones, which will gener-ally need to be refrigerated and used within a few days.

I believe that educating people to make their own cosmetics at home, using fair-trade, home-grown or organic ingredients (wherever possible) is the ideal solution. However this is not necessarily realistic and you may still want to buy ready-made products. If so, take the time to check them out in the following ways.

Things to look out for.

Obviously it is very hard to find any product on the main market that doesn't contain any chemicals. Products without preserva-tives would often have a limited shelf life. A short expiry period does not make a very viable product and is not likely to make you millions.

There are many products that you can buy that contain all natural ingredients, available from specialist shops, health food shops and also online. Of course do check the contents list; don't take 'natural', 'organic' or even 'hypoallergenic' as proof that they are. If you are not sure, write the ingredients down and research them later using reference books or the internet.

It is also good to check the country of manufacture; if it has travelled thousands of miles it is not going to help reduce your carbon footprint. If the packaging has been made using recycled or recyclable materials that, of course, is a bonus.

Although specialist and more 'natural' products may be more expensive than your regular ones, a smaller amount of the product often goes a long, long way, due to the higher concentration of active ingredients.

Here are a few simple recipes to prepare your own products that you can easily follow at home.

159

Recipes.

There are measures you can take to increase the life of all your products. The following tips are for when you want to make your creations last longer than a few days (so don't worry if you're just making a face mask for now).

- Make sure all pots and pans and surfaces are properly cleaned or sterilised.

- Make sure your hands are very clean, or even better, wear gloves.

- Use distilled water if you can; it is important to make sure the ingredients are as pure as possible.

- Keep the finished product in a darkish jar and away from the light or in the fridge.

- Try to avoid using your fingers to get the product out of its container. Use a brush or cotton bud for applying creams or lip balms.

Lip and cheek tint

This is very similar to expensive brands currently available on the high street, but a LOT cheaper!

You will need:

45g raw beetroot
3 tbsp glycerine (usually costs under a pound from Boots or other chemists)

Mix the ingredients in a bowl then place the ingredients in a saucepan of boiling water (or bainmarie) for fifteen minutes.
Strain, put into a glass jar and use sparingly when cooled!

Face masks or packs

There are many quick and simple ways of deep cleansing, revitalising and treating your face.

- *Simply use a whole avocado or banana. Both are highly moisturising and full of vitamins. Mash very well, and apply for five to ten minutes, then wash off. Be careful not to get banana in your hair - it is very difficult to get out!*

- *Tomato is a fantastic ingredient for oily or spotty skin due to its astringent properties and its high concentration of vitamins, including A, C, and E. Simply mash (it may mash better if heated slightly) and apply. You can also add any of the following ingredients: oatmeal, instant potato flakes, fresh mint, brewer's yeast, lemon juice or olive oil.*

- *Cucumber is wonderfully cooling and will tighten your pores and refresh your face. Mash half a cucumber and add two tablespoons of live yogurt and a handful of oats. Apply and rinse off when dry.*

- *Honey has been used for its antiseptic healing and cleansing properties for thousands of years. Add it to yoghurt and banana, yoghurt and carrots (in a blender) or simply paste onto your face after steaming over hot water to open the pores.*

Of course, you can combine any of these ingredients and experiment as much as you like!

The Green Wedding by Suzan St Maur.

We can all be expected to splash out on our big day, but the expenditure of a big white wedding does not need to have a negative impact on the environment. Think about how much goes into planning and producing a wedding. Consider the environmental and ethical costs of a wedding: from the number of invitations you send out to guests (they will probably just be thrown away after), the wastage in the form of leftover food and drink to the electricity used on the big day to light the venue or keep the DJ going. Suzan St Maur offers a number of top tips that the bride and groom can follow to ensure that their wedding is a little more environmentally friendly and ethical.

1. Rings. If buying a new diamond, ensure it was mined in Canada or another fairtrade location. Consider a man-made gemstone instead. For wedding rings, buy secondhand or have new ones made from recycled gold. You can even have wedding rings made from reclaimed wood!

2. Hen and stag celebrations. Organise your party as close to home as possible, and if you are travelling abroad choose overland transport rather than flying. Avoid activities that involve burning fuel or activities that create other forms of pollution.

3. Location. Choose a location that involves minimal travel for you and your guests, and a reception venue that has a decent recycling policy. If you're having a civil wedding, have the ceremony and reception in the same place.

4. Communications. Do as much communication as you can by email or via a wedding website. Ensure that what printed material you do use is on recycled or sustainably sourced paper, using green printing techniques.

5. Wedding dress. Don't buy a brand new dress before checking out dresses to hire, buying secondhand or borrowing and so on. Ensure all wedding outfits, if bought, can be used again afterwards, and choose natural, washable fabrics to avoid the pollution caused by dry cleaning.

6. Wedding gifts. Ask for gifts made from recycled or ethical sources, and remember that money may not be PC but is actually quite green! If you don't need gifts ask guests to make donations to a charity or eco-activity instead.

7. Flowers and floral decorations. Avoid commercial floristry that uses flowers from non-fairtrade countries, imported by air. Try to use organic, locally produced flowers and greenery. Consider potted plants, topiary and dried or fake arrangements instead of cut flowers.

8. Reception. Have yours in daylight hours to cut back on energy used for lighting. Avoid disposable crockery and cutlery; china and metal are greener as they will be reused. Make sure your wedding favours are 'green' in nature, for example, small potted plants. Finally, ensure as much as possible is properly recycled afterwards.

9. Food and drink. Choose organic and locally produced ingredients for your wedding menu wherever possible, ideally using only fresh foods that are in season. There are a number of wedding caterers who specialise in preparing seasonal menus where food is sourced locally. Choose organic, fairtrade, sustainable, biodynamic and British-produced drinks. Ensure your tea and coffee is fairtrade, too.

10. Photography. Ensure your photographer uses digital systems as traditional film involves harsh chemicals. Do not offer guests disposable cameras at your reception. Keep prints to a minimum; allow for online viewing of your pictures wherever possible.

11. Transport. Avoid gas-guzzling cars to transport the wedding party, and try to minimise motor vehicle use amongst guests. Consider horse-drawn transport or pedal power. Alternatively, organise a bus to pick up and transport guests to avoid them bringing their own vehicles.

12. Honeymoon. Remember that the closer to home you honeymoon, in general, the greener it will be. Consider a 'staycation'. If you must go abroad, use a reputable carbon offset scheme and consider a location with eco-tourism. At all costs avoid cruise ships which are normally very 'dirty'.

Shopping by Amanda Hodgson.

We live in a society driven by consumerism. There is so much competition from retailers for our money, but do we ever stop to consider the ethical and environmental implications of our reckless spending? Fruitless spending on cheap clothes from the competitive retailers means we all increase our secondary carbon footprint regularly. But, as Amanda Hodgson explains there is an alternative, we can shop until we drop without wreaking havoc on the world!

The 'secondary carbon footprint' is a term applied to the indirect carbon emissions from the products we use. Stated very simply, your secondary carbon footprint increases with the amount of goods you buy. How to combat this? The answer could be on your doorstep...

Charity shops have never been off the radar of the thrifty and style-conscious, with good reason. I personally view charity shopping as a treasure hunt, with my magpie-eye delighting in extracting the Millen from the Matalan. I have gathered many fortunate finds over my dedicated discount years: a Max Mara cashmere cardigan, Paul Smith fitted jacket and Dunn and co. deerstalker hat to name but a few.

Charity shops are a salve for the conscience and the bank balance. You return home in the black with bulging bags, safe in the knowledge that your purchases have helped some of the world's poorest people and no child has slaved in dire conditions for a meagre wage to satisfy your sartorial desires.

There are rich pickings in Sussex, with charity shop gold on on Blatchington Road and George Street in Hove. The proportion of such establishments is high, offering a diverse range of goods at pleasing prices.

New baby? Look no further than Baby Aid on Blatchington Road, which stocks hardly worn clothes and hardly used toys and equipment for babies and toddlers, with clothes and books for adults too. Oxfam have two shops on this road, a well-organised bookshop with many great titles and rare vinyl. Their clothes shop boasts a good vintage section and suitcases of scarves in pretty patterns.

The YMCA has three shops in the area separating clothes, furniture and electrical goods. The furniture store offers free collection and has a good variety. The YMCA clothes shop also has a selection of china, glassware and jewellery. Nearby, the Martlets have recently opened a new shop selling clothes and furniture.

On George Street is the consistently good Mind shop where I have purchased many a lovely coat. Help the Aged has retro knick-knacks and more unusual vintage clothing. I have rarely left Scope without a bargain, and I can say the same of Barnardo's and the British Heart Foundation. The recently opened Rocking-horse and Samaritans shops are also definitely worth a browse.
Cast your net further and you will find Boundary Road in Portslade, which yields many ultra-cheap wonders. Brighton is good but more expensive, although Traid in the South Lanes have fantastic end of season sales where all stock can be reduced to as little as a pound.

Don't forget that aside from charity shops, all across Sussex there are numerous car boot sales that take place usually at weekends throughout the year. Someone else's junk just may be your gold and through this form of reusing old products you are keeping your secondary carbon footprint low. Check your local Friday Ad for your nearest car boot sale and get shopping!

The Original Hut Company, by Nick and Anna Eastwood.

Where and why it all began.

Last summer we found ourselves in quite an uncomfortable position, I was about to start my maternity leave expecting our second child, and our small marquee business had been hit very hard by the financial downturn.

The only thing keeping us going was our holiday cottage in Camber. Although this was working hard for us it was not enough to support a family. We needed something else but had nothing available to finance further property investment, especially with the mortgage situation being so difficult.

My father-in-law farms in Bodiam, where the land flanks the river Rother and looks out across to Bodiam Castle. We were aware that the 'staycation' was becoming increasing popular and felt we had a site that would suit that type of holiday well. Following a bit of market research we realised that yurts and tipi's were already abundant in the area, and we wanted to be a bit different.

We had realised that many holiday offerings available can have a negative impact on the area around them. The area around us is stunning, and we are so lucky to have the opportunity to enjoy it every day. So we knew that we had to create something that would blend into the environment and have a positive impact upon it rather that the opposite. We were also keen to appeal to those of a similar mindset, feeling that they in turn would have a greater understanding and respect for the countryside. The challenge was set.

The inspiration.

In bygone days, agricultural workers who were working away from the farm were often accommodated in huts: be this a shepherd during lambing, a game keeper on a large estate or a gillie on a valuable stretch of river. There were of course manufactures of huts, but very often these quirky little abodes were fashioned on the farm from surplus materials.

The huts.

Our huts are based on the idea of an old shepherd's hut. What makes them unique is that (in true agricultural fashion) they are built using reclaimed, recycled and locally sourced materials wherever possible. The aim of this is to ensure they have the lowest possible environmental impact. The huts are constructed using old chassis from clapped-out old touring caravans, (this also makes them considerably more manoeuvrable than those on traditional iron wheels), the roofs are made from an old corn or grain bin which would have been left in a farm yard to rust away and the timber for the work tops and seat covers is sourced from sustainable woodland on the farm. The remaining timber used in the construction is all from responsibly farmed forests.

The paint is from 'Farrow and Ball' where all paint is produced using naturally occurring ingredients and pigments. The twelve-volt lighting system is powered via a solar panel on the roof. Storage is supplied using redundant wooden apple boxes. The huts are fitted with tiny little wood-burning stoves, these are fuelled while supply allows with prunings from our own orchards which previously would have been a waste product. All these factors reduced our build cost and continue to reduce the running costs, as well as reusing otherwise redundant materials

During a stay with the Original Hut Company.

Visitors to the huts are also encouraged to recycle as much of their waste as possible. There are the obvious recycling options, such as glass and paper recycling facilities. We also have a worm farm on site to help us process the organic matter into compost. The process of the composting is accelerated by the addition of chicken poo from the hens, which are available to rent for the week. The hens, as well as being good fun, allow children the opportunity to experience firsthand how their food is produced and question the journey it undertakes as it travels from the farm to their plate. To support this we are also working in partnership with other farms and local food producers in order to promote produce from our immediate area.

Areas for further development.

As the site around the huts develops, we intend to add an allotment area where visitors can harvest fruits and vegetables of the season. We are also about to stock up with Fresion bullocks and stock lambs. Although both (unfortunately) are generally considered to be byproducts of modern farming. From these we will from these we will produce meat for both ourselves and the holiday makers.

We have also recently found a supplier of amazing composting loos! (These will be fitted as soon as we can afford them.) They have a solar-powered fan that separates the wet and dry waste, which stops the fermentation process that causes odour. The dried solid waste is stored in sealed containers for six months until it is rendered harmless, then it is used as a composting material. That is probably too much information for most of you, but again it shows how we can use waste to ultimately have a positive effect on the immediate environment.

It's amazing once you raise your level of awareness about waste, the environment around you and what is produced locally. You learn that you can produce so much yourself and that you can live both more cleanly and more cheaply. You find yourself on a roller coaster of sustainable ideals. I love it! Let's hope that a deeper interest in the enviroment is one good thing to come out of this boring, (and depressing) old recession.

With thanks to:
The Original Hut Company. Nick and Anna Eastwood. These unique huts offer a beautiful, comfortable and sustainable boutique camping experience. Set on a farm in the tiny village of Bodiam. The huts offer accommodation for four or five people. Cooking facilities are provided through a gas hob and a fire pit outside, and tiny little woodburners offer cozy and sustainable heating. A separate hut offers piping hot showers toilets and washing facilities. Visit the website for more information www.originalhuts.co.uk or call us on 01580 831 845.

The South Downs joint Committee was formed in 2005 as the result of an agreement entered into by the Countryside Agency (now Natural England) and the fifteen local authorities within the East Hampshire and Sussex Areas of Outstanding Natural Beauty (AONB). In April 2010, the South Downs was designated as a National Park and the AONB status revoked. Between April 2010 and April 2011, the South Downs National Park Authority (SDNPA) will agree its policies and develop its structures. During this transition year, the Joint Committee will continue to work in the former AONBs until 31st March 2011 after which the SDNPA will take on responsibility for managing the newly designated area. See the SDNPA website www.southdowns.gov. uk for further information about the future national park.

Sophie Adler-Mckean is twenty five and has lived in Brighton most of her life. Through various periods of travelling and living abroad, she has emersed herself in other cultures and found herself inspired by different types of natural beauty and healthcare. She is self taught in herbal medicine, homeopathy and natural beauty and continues to increase her knowledge, and make her own products for herself, friends and family in her spare time.If you have any questions regarding the article, or for further information, recipies and tips please contact Sophie at sophiesapothecary@gmail.com.

Suzan St Maur, Green Weddings. Excerpted from 'How To Get Married In Green' by Suzan St Maur (available at all good book shops), http://howtogetmarriedingreen.blogspot.com

Amanda Hodgson is a freelance writer living in Hove. Amanda likes to read, write, bake, sweat it out at yoga and comedy dance to eighties tunes. She believes that sarcasm is the highest form of wit and should be practiced when and whereever possible.

SECTION 9) SUSTAINABLE FUELS

Fossil fuels Vs Alternative fuels by Katie Ramsay.

Most UK car owners run their vehicles on petrol or diesel; fuel that is extracted from crude oil. The burning of oil releases a number of harmful greenhouse gases into the atmosphere. With over twenty eight million of us running around in our cars in the UK,[1] air pollution is an increasing worry. Furthermore, one day our oil supplies will run out, then what?

The majority of us in the UK heat our homes using natural gas. Although it is widely recognised that gas is the cleanest of the fossil fuels it still produces greenhouse gases such as carbon dioxide that damage our atmosphere. If this is not incentive enough to think outside of the box and use alternative fuels to heat your home there is more. Natural gas, like oil and coal is of finite supply. It other words it will run out. Around the world we are rapidly depleting our reserves of gas, oil and coal. The time has come for us to start using alternative fuels to secure our futures.

Here we will look at alternatives to fossil fuels and demonstrate how we do not need to rely on fossil fuels in Sussex.

---

1   Crown Copyright: ONS http://www.dft.gov.uk/adobep
     df/162469/221412/221552/228052/458127/vehiclelicensing2008.pdf

Heating the Home.

Picture the scene: it's a freezing evening; you arrive home from work to a warm house, radiators on… It is something that we all take for granted; heat. But what are we going to do to combat the negative effects of burning gas on our environment and what will we do when it runs out?

It is important for us to find alternatives to burning fossil fuels for obvious environmental reasons, but also for reasons of practicality. How can we continue to rely on fuels that we know are not renewable? It is important for us to look at more sustainable alternatives.

We do not need to rely on natural gas. There are other alternatives that we can use alone or combine with natural gas to heat our homes.

Alternatives to fossil fuels.

There are a number of alternative energy sources that can be used to heat your home or provide it with electricity. More specifically, solar power (yes, even in the UK), geothermal resources, biomass and wood are all alternative resources that you can use to heat your home. I could spend pages discussing all the viable alternatives to fossil fuels, but instead I am going to focus on a traditional source of energy that is often overlooked; wood. I will explore the debate of wood versus natural gas as a resource for heating your home.

A lot of people have a fireplace in their homes. Think of all your family and friends. How many of them have an open fire place in their living room? How many of them use it as an aid to heating

their homes and how many use it as a design feature?

I am sure that very few people take advantage of their open fire place. My friends cite reasons such as; 'I can't be bothered to get the chimney swept' or 'it's not safe' as excuses against using wood to heat their homes. To dispel fact from fiction I have prepared a brief pros and cons list for using wood to heat your home instead of natural gas.

There are a number of positives that come from burning wood: it is competitively priced, it is convenient and accessible, it is good for conservation of forests and encouraging biodiversity through management of eco systems in the forests.[1] However, when presenting an alternative to fossil fuels there are a number of factors that I believe are especially important to discuss.

Renewable Energy.

When weighing up the pros and cons of wood burning as an alternative means of heating your home, the first and main thing that springs to my mind as a positive is that wood is a renewable source of energy.

---

1   Crown Copyright 200: http://www.forestry.gov.uk/forestry/INFD-839EC6#Woodfuel5

Carbon Neutral.

Another vital heading under the pros list of the wood versus gas debate is that burning wood is claimed to be carbon neutral. The carbon dioxide that is released when you burn wood is re-absorbed by the trees that have grown in its place. The Forestry Commission stresses the importance of burning wood that originates from a sustainable managed forest. 'Woodfuel produced in sustainable managed forests is "replaced" by the next crop of growing trees, which re absorbs the same amount of carbon that is emitted by the current crop being burned.'[1]

Whether the wood is burnt or not, when a tree decomposes in its natural environment, for example in the forest, it will release the carbon that it absorbed during its lifetime back into the environment. As the Forestry Commission explains, regardless of how many trees we grow forests will always end up as carbon

---

1   Crown Copyright 2010: http://www.forestry.gov.uk/forestry/INFD-839EC6#Woodfuel5

neutral; as the dying trees release carbon the new trees absorb it.[1] As woodheat.org aptly put it; 'trees recycle carbon dioxide, wood burning just warms you, not the globe.'[2]

These ideals are very well in theory but in practice to get the environmental benefits from burning wood it is important to remember a few key points.

- It is important to buy wood that is certified by the Forest Stewardship Council (FSC) or from a supplier who maintains a relationship with the Forestry Commission in the UK. There are a number of reasons to support the Forest Stewardship Council. Among those, it ensures that all wood bearing its seal of approval has been replaced with new trees or that a forest has been able to regenerate naturally.[3]
- Burn wood correctly. Certain types of wood burn more efficiently than others. If you burn the wrong wood then it will be a waste of energy and then it won't be as environmentally friendly.

1   Crown Copyright 2010: http://www.forestry.gov.uk/forestry/infd-7qglzg#Q7
2   Copyright woodheat.org: http://www.woodheat.org/why/10good.htm
3   Courtesy of FSC Forest Stewardship Council, A.C :http://www.fsc-uk.org/?page_
       id=11

Different types of wood for burning.

We spoke to Nick Harris from Four Seasons Fuel in Billingshurst to get the low down about the different types of woods for burning.

All firewood burns better when seasoned and some burns better when split rather than burnt as whole logs. Here is a list of different kinds of woods that you may be interested in...[1]

- Apple and pear, burns slowly and steadily with little flame but good heat. The scent is also pleasing.

- Ash, the best wood for burning, providing plenty of heat (will also burn green).

- Beech and hornbeam, good when well seasoned.

- Birch, good heat and a bright flame, burns quickly.

- Blackthorn and hawthorn, very good for burning. Burns slowly but with good heat

- Cherry, also burns slowly with good heat and a pleasant scent.

- Cypress, burns well but fast when seasoned, and may spit.

- Hazel, good, but hazel has so many other uses so hopefully you won't have to burn it!

---

1   www.fourseasonsfuel.co.uk

- Holly, good when well seasoned.

- Horse Chestnut, good flame and heating power but spits a lot.

- Larch, fairly good for heat but crackles and spits.

- Maple, good all rounder for burning.

- Oak, very old dry seasoned oak is excellent, burning slowly with a good heat.

- Pine, burns well with a bright flame but crackles and spits.

- Poplar, avoid all poplar wood; it burns very slowly with little heat. This is why poplar wood is used to make matchsticks.

- Willow, very good for burning. In fact there is a growing interest in biomass production of coppiced willow as a fuel.

Seasoned firewood.
Seasoned wood is much better for burning than unseasoned fire wood. Seasoning usually means leaving the wood for a period of time in the right conditions. Leaving wood in storage, enables a reduction of the water or moisture content. Freshly-cut wood can be up to forty five to fifty per cent water, while well-seasoned fire-wood generally has twenty to thirty per cent moisture content. Well-seasoned firewood can also be a lot easier to light. It will produce more heat and burns cleaner. It can also be smokeless.

Burning unseasoned wood.
You could try burning green wood; however you will need a lot of heat to dry the wood, thus burning green wood is not very

energy efficient. The result is less heat per KW into your home and will process a lot of acidic water from the wood, this will form creosote that will stick to your chimney or eat into your chimney lining. This may lead to a chimney fire. Unseasoned wood will burn slowly with very little heat, your chimney flue will not heat up adequately.

Seasoned firewood will burn hotter, pushing heat up the flue and will create a faster draw. This means that the small amount of vapour from the water content of your seasoned firewood will push directly upwards and will not condense on your chimney flue.

Seasoning firewood .
All trees contain thousands of microscopic water tubes that carry water from the small base roots (the larger roots are for keeping the tree in the ground). The smaller roots carry water to the leaves and new shoots. These tubes can stay full of water for many years after they have been felled; seasoning the wood will dry these water tubes making the firewood ready for use.

It is also worth pointing out what types of wood you shouldn't burn; Nick chides us on some common faux pas…

Wood you shouldn't burn in your home.
Yes we have all done it… Burning MDF, chipboard, floor boards, treated and painted woods are not a good idea. In doing this you are potentially damaging your health plus the environment due to the chemicals that are layered in the wood. 'You have been warned.'

I hope that from presenting this positive case supporting wood burning as an alternative to gas and electricity you will all call in the chimney sweep and get in the logs.

But before you do it is important to understand that burning wood is not suitable for everyone.

Smoke controlled areas.

Think back to 1952, London and 'The Big Smoke'. A mixture of air pollution caused for the most part by coal burning fires combined with weather conditions, gave London its famous synonym. After the 'Great Smog', legislation was brought in to regulate air pollution in the UK. Variations of this act remain in force today controlling what we can and cannot burn. Burning wood does not have the same negative implications as burning coal but nevertheless in many parts of the UK that are designated 'smoke controlled areas,' where you are not legally allowed to burn wood domestically.

So, when debating whether to switch to burning biomass or wood as an alternative to, or combined with gas or electric heating, you need to first consider your location and whether you fall into a 'smoke controlled area' (SCA). SCAs are determined by Local Authorities in response to the Clean Air Act of 1993. The Local Authority has the power to control the production of domestic and industrial smoke within its boundaries.[1]

I live in a smoke controlled area – what can I do?

If you live in a SCA then; 'It is an offence to emit smoke from a chimney of a building, from a furnace or from any fixed boiler.' This offence is punishable by an 1000 pound fine.[2] You can consider the use of an exempt appliance or smokeless fuels. Smokeless fuels are those that can be burnt in an open fireplace and not emit smoke. Likewise, an exempt appliance is one that has

1   Crown Copyright: http://smokecontrol.defra.gov.uk/background.php
2   Crown Copyright: http://smokecontrol.defra.gov.uk/background.php

passed testing to ensure that it is capable of burning a smoke-less fuel without emitting smoke, there is extensive information about this available from Defra.[1]

SCAs in Sussex.

If you live within the perimeters of Brighton and Hove City Council then you need to check whether you fall into the catchment area of a SCA, as much of the city centre and surrounding urban areas are smoke free zones. The same goes with Lewes District Council. Further afield Eastbourne BC, Hastings BC, Worthing BC, Chichester DC, Mid Sussex DC and the Arun DC areas do not currently impose any restrictions regarding domestic smoke emissions. However, it is advisable to clarify this with your local council before sparking up your open fire or wood burner as this is to the prerogative of your local authority.

I have demonstrated that in a time when the world is panicking about dwindling supplies of fossil fuels, there is another way and an alternative, renewable resource that you can rely on to heat your homes.

Sam Rose from Green Man and Van discusses our options for replacing the oil that we rely on so heavily with a renewable and more eco-friendly alternative in the world of transport.

---

1   Crown Copyright: http://smokecontrol.defra.gov.uk/background.php

Renewable resources by Sam Rose.

Traditional sources.

Fuel sources for motor vehicles are traditionally made from fossil fuels that consist of deposits from once living organisms and take many centuries to form. Oil is a liquid fossil fuel that is formed from the remains of marine micro organisms deposited on the sea floor. After millions of years the deposits end up in rock and sediment where oil is trapped in small spaces. It can be extracted by large drilling platforms.[1] The crude oil is then refined for a variety of uses including the petrol and diesel used in most vehicles.

Environmental issues.

When oil is burned it produces large amounts of carbon dioxide, which is released into the atmosphere. As discussed in section one, carbon dioxide is a greenhouse gas, which means that it absorbs the infrared radiation omitted by living organisms on planet earth and reflects some of it back towards the surface. This is the same effect that occurs in a greenhouse, hence the term greenhouse effect. Increases in CO2 emissions will lead to an increase in the earth's temperature, otherwise known as global warming.

---

1   Copyright: Stephanie Enzler 2006 www.lenntech.com http://www.lenntech.com/greenhouse-effect/fossil-fuels.htm#ixzz0fcSLydF9

Alternatives.

Recently, the exposure global warming has received and the perception that it is getting worse has led to demands for a reduction in carbon dioxide emissions. Coupled with falling global oil supplies, scientists, governments and corporations have begun to look into alternative fuels or methods of powering transportation.

Lithium-ion battery.

These are light weight high efficiency batteries similar to the ones already used in laptops and mobile phones. The motor industry has turned to these batteries as they are seen as an efficient, potential solution to dwindling oil supplies. There are examples of lithium-ion batteries in hybrid car models from Ford, Toyota, Honda and Lexus among others.

Bolivia is known to have some of the most plentiful supplies of lithium underneath salt flats in the southern plains. However, as is the case with fossil fuels lithium is a limited resource and many believe that within a fairly short period of time, as it is increasingly used in the transport industry, supplies will dwindle. There are also environmental concerns surrounding lithium extraction. The most cost-effective method of extracting lithium is evaporating brine in special ponds lined with toxic plastic. Lithium is corrosive and breathing its dust can irritate the nose and throat. In big doses it can cause fluid build-up in the lungs.[1]

Hydrogen fuel cell.

Hydrogen has the advantage of potentially being a renewable

---

1   Jim Motavalli, Driving Directions blog: http://www.thedailygreen.com/living-green/ blogs/cars-transportation/lithium-batteries-electric-cars-460209

energy source, depending on how it is produced. It is not naturally occurring and must be extracted from other sources; these include fossil fuels such as natural gas or petrol and from water through electrolysis. Obviously fossil fuels are not a renewable resource and extracting hydrogen this way ultimately contributes to global carbon dioxide emissions. However, if hydrogen is extracted from water and done so in an environmentally friendly way, 'from a renewable source such as solar, wind, biomass, wave, tidal, geothermal or hydropower then there is the potential to produce hydrogen sustainably in a nonpolluting manner.'[1]

In transportation, fuel cells are used to create electricity that power electric motors, using either hydrogen or a reformed hydrocarbon fuel together with oxygen from the atmosphere.

At the moment hydrogen cells made in a sustainable way are inefficient because it costs more to produce hydrogen than is earned by using hydrogen in fuel cells.

Liquid petroleum gas (LPG).

The main advantage of using liquid petroleum gas is that it is a by product of the refining of crude oil. It currently provides about three per cent of the energy consumed, and burns cleanly with no soot and very few sulphur emissions, posing no ground or water pollution hazards.

LPG has a lower energy density than either petrol or diesel, so the equivalent fuel consumption is higher. Carbon dioxide emissions from burning LPG are also far lower than those from more traditional fossil fuels. However it is obviously still a derivative of a refined fossil fuel and as such is not sustainable.

Biodiesel.

Biodiesels are made from plant oils or crop wastes and can be used to run diesel engines. Burning these fuels simply returns to the atmosphere the carbon that plants extracted while they were growing.[1] One of the major advantages of biofuel or biodiesel is that it can be used without modification to existing diesel engines.

Types of Biodiesel.

There are three main sources of biodiesel.

i)   Biodiesel made from imported oil, such as palm oil.
ii)   Biodiesel made from crops grown in this country, such as oil seed rape.
iii)   Biodiesel made from recycled oil used by restaurants, pubs, cafes and so on.

---

1   Copyright George Monibot http://www.monbiot.com/archives/2004/11/23/feeding-cars-not-people/

The use of the first two types listed here can be problematic. The first type often leads to:

- mass deforestation in order that the land can be used for cultivating oil palm for processing into biofuel.
- Forced displacement of small farmers from their land.
- Poor labour rights.
- Food price hikes.

Biofuel production is not always the main problem in these cases but it is often a major contributory factor.[1]

The problem with growing crops such as oil seed rape in the UK or soya beans in the US, specifically for conversion to and use as biofuel, is that the land used to grow them would be more efficiently and effectively used for food cultivation. In 2004 Guardian columnist George Monbiot calculated that 'switching to green fuels requires four and half times our arable area. Even the EU's more modest target of twenty per cent by 2020 would consume almost all our cropland.'[2]

Why we use biodiesel made from recycled cooking oil.

There are several advantages of using Biodiesel that has been made from recycled cooking oil. The main one of these is its use of a waste product that is otherwise very difficult to dispose of. On a large scale it is not a solution to providing enough fuel for the whole of this country's transport industry. However, production levels could be substantially increased through improved collection and recycling systems. Aside from the environmental

---

1   Copyright Christan Aid August 2009: http://www.christianaid.org.uk/images/biofuels-report-09.pdf

2   Copyright George Monibot http://www.monbiot.com/archives/2004/11/23/feeding-cars-not-people/

advantages of using biodiesel there are also currently economic and mechanical benefits. Currently biodiesel has a reduced duty of twenty pence per litre (from the 1st April 2010 this only applied to biodiesel made from recycled cooking oil) and is therefore cheaper than mineral diesel by about ten to fifteen pence per litre.

There are also mechanical benefits from using biodiesel due to its lubricity. Use of biodiesel reduces long-term wear on engines to less than half that which has been observed on engines running on petro diesel.[1]

We currently buy our diesel from Four Seasons Fuel based in Coneyhurst just outside Billingshurst (www.fourseasonsfuel.co.uk) and currently pay ninety nine pence per litre.

---

1   Copyright CytoCulture International, Inc.:http://www.cytoculture.com/Biodies el%20Handbook.htm#ENGINE%20PERFORMANCE

With thanks to.

Katie Ramsay.

Nick Harris and Four Seasons Fuels. Four Seasons Fuel is family run business with three generations in the firewood industry, employing eight hard working staff hoping to bring a personal and dedicated professional service to the general public.

They have invested in the most up to date firewood machinery on the market, to bring you the finest cut logs to put into your fireplace.

Four Seasons Fuels are one of the few online firewood/log stores which source their firewood locally from all over Sussex and Surrey.
http://www.fourseasonsfuel.co.uk/

Sam Rose. The Green Man and Van is an environmentally aware and socially responsible removal and logistics company based in London and Brighton. Our aim is to offer friendly and reliable services that have minimal impact on the environment. Our vehicles are modern, clean, and fully insured. They are fuelled with locally sourced biodiesel, made from recycled waste cooking oil. 020 3086 9775 sam@greenmanandvan.co.uk www.greenmanandvan.co.uk

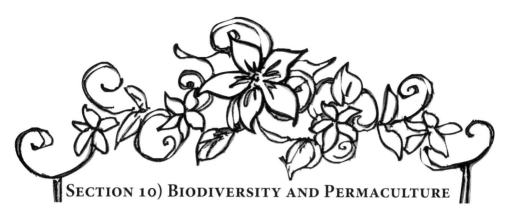

**Biodiversity and Sustainability - two sides of the same coin
By Dr Dan Danahar.**

The great flood of humanity.

It was perhaps the efforts of Noah and his family that represented humanity's first attempt to save biodiversity from the great floods that covered the surface of the earth. Now, in 2010, the designated International Year of Biodiversity, we are strongly reminded of Noah's labours, only this time the flood is composed of the relentless rise in human population and it is humanity itself that possesses the greatest threat to biodiversity today.

If you were born in the 1950's you're a member of the first generation of humans to see global population double during your lifetime.[1] Currently world population is believed to be at a little fewer than seven billion people and some estimates suggest that by 2054 it will reach nine billion.[2] Every new human is a new mouth to feed and a new person to provide resources for.

Of course population increases are not the same all over the world. In Britain the population rose from 52.4 million in mid-1960

---

1   Wilson, E. O. (2008) The Future of Life, Abacus, London.

2   Copyright UN The World at Six Billion: http://www.un.org/esa/population/publica tions/sixbillion/sixbilpart1.pdf

to 61.4 million in mid-2008 (an increase of just over seventeen per cent), whereas, the West African country of Ghana has gone from between 6.8 to 23.4 million during the same period (an increase of 244.1 per cent).[1]

Consequently, Ghana has seen a massive increase in the removal of it's native rainforest, so that more land can be converted for agricultural purposes. The removal of the forests leads to the loss of all the unique species of plants animals and other organisms that they contain. Now only fifteen per cent of this forest remains intact. Of this fifteen per cent not all is good quality rainforest and if you travel through Ghana as I have, you will see the relentless train of trucks still taking tropical hardwood trees out to be turned into coffins, doors or beds, which are all common sights by the side of the road. Ironically, it's in tropical countries, like Ghana, where the majority of the earth's biodiversity exists.

But why is biodiversity such an important issue if there are people's livelihoods at stake? To answer this we need to start by asking what it is biodiversity?

1   http://www.google.com/publicdata?ds=wb-wdi&met=sp_pop_totl&tdim=true&dl=e
     n&hl=en&q=world+population+data#met=sp_pop_totl&idim=country:GHA:GBR

What is biological diversity?

Fundamentally, biological diversity or biodiversity as it has become known is the rich variety of living things that we find on the Earth. But when we use the term biodiversity it begs the question, what form of biological diversity are we looking at? Clearly natural habitats vary one from another. A wildflower meadow is obviously very different to that of a tropical forest or a coral reef. So clearly at the habitat level there is considerable biological diversity, but then there are the species: birds; mammals; amphibians; reptiles; invertebrates; flowering plants; fungi and so on. The list is almost inexhaustible. Species show an almost infinite amount of diversity in form and function. Furthermore, there is the genetic diversity, the endlessly varied chains of DNA, which are made up from mind bogglingly complex sequences of genes.

To date it has been suggested that species are the common currency of biodiversity.[1] This is because in a very real sense they are tangible, something you can pick up with your own hands, in the vast majority of cases. For centuries now naturalists have been recording species either by simply logging their occurrence or by collecting specimens and returning them to our great museums, where they have been classified, catalogued and stored. Ecologists call the number of species found in a habitat the species richness and this simple index is now widely used as the most common measure of biodiversity.

---

1   Spicer, J. I. (2006) Biodiversity: a beginners guide, Oneworld publications, Oxford.

Does biodiversity play a role?

If you have children the likelihood is that at some point you will have helped them with their science homework on food chains. Food chains and webs are made up of species, each species transferring its energy to the next species in the chain. By and large, it is the food webs and the non-living habitats in which they exist that make up the ecosystems of the world. Ecosystems are incredibly complex and this leads them to develop 'emergent properties', unpredictable outcomes of this very complexity.

Have you ever looked at an insect walking on the ground and asked what its purpose is? Let's consider a moth caterpillar as an example: it will start life as an egg which hatches into a caterpillar, followed by a change into a chrysalis and finally it emerges as a moth and when the moth finds a mate the cycle will start all over again.

However, when the caterpillar eats a leaf it will leave holes in the foliage and thus allow extra light to reach further into the habitat, giving other organisms the benefit of the additional illumination, perhaps a germinating seed. When the caterpillar processes its food, the frass it drops (the scientific word for caterpillar dung)

may enrich the nutrient levels of the spot in which it lands, thus enhancing the conditions for some fungi to grow. As an adult moth, feeding on the nectar produced in one flower and then the next, it may transfer pollen and enable new seed to form, and it may pick up a pseudo scorpion hitchhiker transferring it from one location to the next and so aiding its locomotory difficulties. Finally if the moth doesn't die of old age or a disease or parasite infestation, it may form the part of the diet of a bat, a bird, or some other organism. Indeed this may become the outcome at any stage in its life cycle.

Each individual life form has the potential to play multiple roles and so as their life cycles turn season on season, year on year, like cogs in some great biological mechanism, they each make their contribution to the functioning ecosystems they inhabit. However, unlike ancient clockwork devices designed to calculate precise outcomes, the results of interactions between species within ecosystems is very much harder to predict. It is the complexity of these interactions that leads to the emergent properties that scientists call ecosystem services.

Human beings rely on a host of invisible services that ecosystems provide. For example: they provide foods, medicines and fuels; they regulate climate, waste disposal, the purification of clean air and water, crop pollination, pest and disease control and they lock up carbon; they support seed dispersal, nutrient recycling and dispersal, and the process of photosynthesis that ultimately provides the mechanism for all the primary production within ecosystems. They preserve genetic diversity and provide recreation for all of us. This is in addition to the opportunities for scientific discovery, cultural, intellectual and spiritual inspiration.

An example that demonstrates the significance of these services is that of the watershed beneath the Catskill Mountains in New York State. Over the preceding hundred and fifty years natural forest had been systematically removed to produce farmland. When in the 1990's the New York City water supply began to deteriorate, the city faced the option between investing eight billion US dollars in a new water treatment facility or one and a half billion US dollars to restore and replant the forests and thus return the natural purification services to the watershed. In this case the economic imperative made it clear to perceive the true value of this ecosystem service.[1]

Biodiversity and economics.

It is only in the last couple of decades that economists have started to appreciate the significant role biodiversity plays in providing these services.[2] The Economics of Ecosystem and Bio-diversity (TEEB) study is now a major international partnership designed to focus attention on the global economic benefits of biodiversity. During 2009 the first report that outlined the current problems was published and in 2010 the second phase report is to be published that is purported to make suggestions of how these difficulties can be addressed. The general view now is that there is a need to reset the economic compass. Our species live on one planet, but we have been living as if we have the resources of multiple planets. We need to learn to value nature for its true worth, before its too late.[3]

---

1   Reproduced by permission from Macmillan Publishers Ltd: [Nature] (Chichilnisky, G. and G. Heal. 1998. Economic returns from the biosphere. 391: 629-630), copy right (1998)

2   Balmford A. et al. (2002) Economic Reasons for Conserving Wild Nature, Science, Vol 297, 950-953.

3   The home of TEEB on the web: http://www.teebweb.org

Mass extinction.

Globally the loss of species has been accelerating in line with human population increase. For some species, loss and extinction is a natural process. Scientists who have studied fossil records have discovered there have been five mass extinctions during geological history. The last, approximately sixty five million years ago, occurred when the dinosaurs ruled the earth and is now widely accepted as the consequence of a massive asteroid strike in the Gulf of Mexico. Estimates of the general background extinction rates have been calculated from the fossil record and although opinion varies, comparisons with the contemporary situation suggest an increase in species loss of fifty to 10,000 greater than that of the background rate. We are currently destroying biodiversity at an alarming rate. These losses are irretrievable, deprive us all and damage the very life support systems we all rely upon. Many scientists now believe that they have accumulated enough evidence to support the contention that we are approaching the sixth great mass extinction.

How many species can we lose?

So how many species can we lose before we irreparably damage our planetary life support system? Nobody really knows but there are many predictions. Some ecologists believe that if we lose a species from a particular ecosystem, then there are others that will take over its functional role.

Other ecologists have postulated what's called the rivet hypothesis. Imagine you are flying on an aircraft; perhaps you are just taking a sip from your gin and tonic and as you look through the window, at the wing outside, you see a tiny rivet break loose and fly away. Mildly distressing, your mellowed state of mind is momentarily disturbed. However, it's only one rivet you tell yourself, but then another rivet flies off, followed by another and another. You know that eventually there will be the proverbial rivet that breaks the aircraft's back. Many ecologists believe that ecosystems may behave in a similar way, in that it will collapse if too many species are removed. Interestingly, the analogy holds fast a little further, when you consider that whilst on an aircraft, your atmosphere and internal climate is regulated by the aircraft, you're supplied with food and drink and your waste is dealt with.[1]

Finally, many other ecologists agree on the idea of keystone species, which like the keystones in the arches above doorways, are essential for the maintenance of the structure of an ecological community. The theory goes that if the keystone species within an ecosystem become extinct, like the keystones being removed from an archway, the structures will collapse. A classic example of a keystone species is that of the sea otter that maintains the luxuriant kelp beds of the north eastern Pacific Ocean and southern Bering Sea, by feeding on the sea urchins that would otherwise decimate the kelp.[2]

1   Ehrlich, P. and A. Ehrlich (1981) The rivet poppers. Extinction: The Causes and Con sequences of the Disappearance of Species. New York, Random House

2   Estes, James E.; Norman S. Smith, John F. Palmisano (1978). "Sea otter predation and community organization in the Western Aleutian Islands, Alaska". Ecology 59 (4):822–833

It is undisputed that a large amount of the world's terrestrial eco systems have already been transformed by human action and ultimately as human population continues to rise, this could lead to one of two possible scenarios. Either keystone species will become extinct and the planet will suffer ecosystem collapse leading to the sixth mass extinction, or the earth's biodiversity will become increasingly impoverished, so that when you travel from one part of the planet to another you will only ever see the same species of animals and plants, the weeds that can cope with what humans do to their environment.

2010, The International Year of Biodiversity (IYB).

The first time the term 'biodiversity' really registered in the public consciousness was when the governments of the world came together at the Rio Earth Summit in 1992, to talk about world development issues and more specifically the environment. It was at the Rio summit that the Convention on Biological Diversity (CBD) was set up (as part of the United Nations Environment Programme) and to date there are 193 signatory countries who have joined the treaty. The CBD was set up to reduce the loss of species and in 2002 the United Nations produced targets to significantly reduce the loss of species by 2010. Europe went one step further and agreed to halt species loss by the same date.

Of course humans are part of this biodiversity too and have the power to protect it but unfortunately, as expressed by Dr Ahmed Djoghlaf, Executive Secretary, of the CBD, at the launch of IYB at the Natural History Museum in London, 'The CBD has failed quite miserably'. So the eighth Secretary-General of the United Nations, Ban Ki-moon, suggested that we celebrate 2010. And so 2010 has become the International Year of Biodiversity. So how can we celebrate IYB?

Biophobia.

If we want to make any progress with the idea that biodiversity has to be saved, humanity has to learn to value it. As a school-teacher I have spent a lot of my life saying to children when they discover a new species of animal from the school pond, 'No not Err, its Wow!' Because invariably 'Err' is the first thing to come out of their mouths when they look at the creature. It's a thoughtless response but one that tells us so much about the way in which we have alienated ourselves and our offspring from the natural world. Take spiders for instance, no native species of spider has ever caused the death of an individual in the UK but so many people have an irrational abhorrence of them. One thing is for sure more spiders have been killed by humans than any number of humans have been killed by spiders, which when you think about it, is insane because we depend so greatly on spiders to control the pests that feed on our crops. Our culture does not accept the prejudice associated with homophobia, sexism or racism, so why tolerate the prejudice associated with speciesism, the widespread discrimination that is practiced by humans against other species? We need to get over such phobias and to do this we must engage the public more.

Bioliteracy.

We need to encourage people to become interested in biodiversity and the wildlife around them. To be bio-literate means to be aware of local biodiversity, the same way stock-brokers are aware of the stocks and shares on the stock exchange. Biodiversity is our livelihood. One way to do this is to become more familiar with individual species, to find time to watch them, to learn to identify them, to live with them in harmony. All species are as much the syllabic nuclei of biodiversity as words are the foundation of any language. Let me put it another way:

TRY NOT TO READ THESE WORDS.

If you can read English it's virtually impossible to look at any words without comprehending their meaning. So what if it was in some other language that you can't read, like Chinese? Then the information would be concealed until you became familiar with Chinese. Reading the natural world is pretty much the same thing; we have become so unattached to our local environment that we no longer have any real sense of how to read it.

Becoming familiar with local biodiversity is rather like learning to read. In Brighton and Hove we run a citizen's science project called the Big Biodiversity Butterfly Count. (BBBC). It encourages members of the public to take their first biodiversity reading lesson. An ABC to biodiversity if you like, because if you can't, read how can you be adequately informed about what's happening in your world? Members of the public, school children, anybody who can pick up a leaflet, can identify their local butterflies and send the data online to the BBBC team.

Butterflies are great indicators of environmental change because they are easy to identify, there are currently only forty five species in the Sussex. They are sensitive creatures too, dependent on subtle changes in microclimate, habitat structure and so on, as are most insects.

So by identifying and recording butterflies we hope to make two gains:

1. Increased knowledge about year on year changes to our local environment and…

2. An increasingly bioliterate populace, a community that values the natural world more that it currently does.

This is a shift from the apocalyptic view; it's a case of the glass half full, not half empty. It's about engaging individuals and empowering them to do something positive in their own part of the world. It really is a case of thinking globally and acting locally. If their interest in recording wildlife grows, they can become involved in one of the more serious recording schemes lead by a host of other organisations. For example, the national charity Butterfly Conservation working in conjunction with a series of other organisations, has encouraged volunteers to record butterflies since 1970. The data this has yielded has been invaluable in allowing scientists to monitor trends in butterfly numbers, which reflect changes in the environment.

Good news stories - the Dorothy Stringer butterfly haven.

I'd like to end on a positive note. All too often we hear scare stories about the loss of habitats, mostly at a global level. We rarely hear about the success stories and the people who are actually doing things to make a difference. At the school which I work at, we converted a 0.4 hectare piece of amenity grassland, with a total list of twelve wildflower species in its sward, to one that now has 107 species. This was achieved in two years. This site has gone from zero to nine breeding species of butterfly and now hosts ninety species of beetle and other rare and endangered species. This was not a difficult thing to do; it was just something that required a little imagination.

Sustainability is the left hand of biodiversity and biodiversity is the right hand of sustainability. They are the two sides are of the same coin. Sustainable living, living as if we have just the one planet to live on, makes a lot more sense once you understand a little more about biodiversity and why it's important.

Permaculture by Beth Tilston.

What is permaculture? Ask ten people and you'll get ten different answers. 'It's a design system.' 'It's a way of letting nature teach us how to grow.' 'It's a way of designing sustainable human settlements.' 'It's a radical approach to food production.' My favourite description of permaculture is that it is 'applied common sense'. Often, when you hear about an example of permaculture - for example a gardener using the heat produced when compost decomposes to keep his greenhouse warm - it seems at once both strikingly innovative and blindingly obvious. Permaculture techniques like this are innovative, but permacultural innovation doesn't spring from nowhere, it comes about through long, detailed observation.

The term 'permaculture' was coined by Bill Mollison and David Holmgren in Australia in the 1970s. Many of the principles stemmed from the close observation of nature, thus, permaculture originally came from a conflation of the words 'permanent' and 'agriculture'. As the practice developed it became clear that permaculture was applicable beyond the confines of agriculture and it came to mean 'permanent culture' in general. It wasn't invented by Mollison and Holmgren though. People have been using permaculture techniques to some degree for millenia, so rather than a new and innovative way of thinking, it's really very very old.

Permaculture ethics.

The backbone of permaculture is its ethics. These can be summed up in one handy (and rhyming!) phrase; 'earth care, People care, fair shares'. Earth care refers to making sure that you think explicitly about the effect of what you do on the earth and the living things upon it. It means working with and for nature rather than against it. Many of the actions that people are taking to combat climate change would fall into this category: cycling instead of driving, eating locally and so on.

Acknowledging that people matter forms the basis of the 'people care' ethic. It's not about prioritising people over the planet, or the planet over people; it's about realising that we are part of the planet! On a macro scale, this ethic means thinking about the care of all people across the world. This will have implications for the way that we, in rich countries, live our lives, replacing resource hungry systems which take away from people in poorer countries with more sustainable systems.

Fair shares is about thinking how much we are consuming and producing and reconciling these things with the needs of other people and the earth. It's about not taking too much and giving back more. It's the ethic that recognises that we live on a finite planet, with finite resources and we need to be careful about what we use.

Permaculture principles.

The ethics sound very worthy and philosophical - a good way of living our lives - but you can't design a garden from them, right? That's where the permaculture 'principles' come in. The principles are what will guide your overall design. Different permaculture 'schools' will teach you varying principles, but the ones below are a good overview.

Use natural patterns. Nature doesn't do unnecessary work, so learn from nature what needs to be done and what doesn't. This might mean something like instigating a no-dig system on your plot. As an experiment, take a walk in the countryside which includes some farmed land and a wood. Take a good look at the soil in both of these places and compare the two. Often, the soil on farmed land is very thin and unhealthy. Around Brighton there are places where vertically ploughed fields are down to the chalk in places. Compare this with the thick, rich soil of the wood and see what can be learnt about mulching, about cycling nutrients, about not disturbing the flora and fauna of the soil. Nature has something to teach us about the world beyond the garden too. For example, in winter most plants and animals slow down or even become dormant. The trees lose their leaves and you can really see their workings, their bones. Try using winter as a time for slowing down and thinking, for looking at the bones of things.

Work with, not against nature. This starts with taking a long hard look at what's there. When you're doing a permaculture design in a landscape, the advice is that you spend a year in observation. That's not a year sitting on your bottom and doing nothing. It's a year spent looking at where the shade falls and the frost settles; a year watching what plants come up where; a year to discover the direction of the prevailing wind and whether or not you have frogs in your pond. You might be itching to get on with things, but the year of observation is not only necessary, it's fun. It's during the observation period that you can experience the joy of watching a shrub burst into bud, a bee collecting pollen or the eureka moment when a crucial connection is made. When you know your landscape like the back of your hand, then the more detailed planning can come in. Working with nature means planting willow for fuel or basketry in that boggy patch you have rather than using energy and resources to drain it and grow vegetables. Think about what you have on your land and how it can be used in your design as it is, rather than trying to change it to suit yourself.

Use diversity. Polycultures are more productive, more stable and more resilient  than monocultures. Think about maximising the number of different things that you grow. Can you plan so that your land is productive all through the year and you have many different types of produce?

Important functions to be supported by many components. From an agricultural point of view, just growing one thing is a risky business. Think about the Irish potato famine. If you have a critical function - like growing food or earning money - make sure that you are supporting this from many different angles. Take a look at your income streams. Are you reliant on one job to provide for you? What if you lose this job? Think about spreading out the way you earn money over a number of different endeavours.

Multi-function. You can't afford to have things in your design that only do one thing. Think about the compost example given earlier. The compost is decomposing and will eventually be used to grow plants, but while it does so it is producing the output of heat which can be used to raise the temperature of your greenhouse. Given observation and thought, there are probably lots of other functions for your compost as well. A good guideline is that everything should perform at least three functions.

Maximise beneficial relationships. Slugs are bad, right? Not if you are a frog or a duck. Put a pond near to your growing space so that you benefit from these marvellous creatures and they benefit from you. Another example of maximising beneficial relationships is the 'three sisters' planting practiced by several Native American tribes. This involves planting corn, beans and squash together. In theory, the corn makes a support for the beans, the squash acts as a mulch and the beans are a nitrogen fixer. The beans will finish first, then the corn is harvested and the squash can spread themselves out in the space that's left. The permaculture idea of zoning fits into the principle of maximising beneficial relationships. Zoning means putting the things that need the most attention where you are more likely to see them often and the things that need less attention further away. You might put your salad crops near your back door because you're likely to pay more attention to them there and plant your orchard - which needs much less input - away from the house.

Cycling and recycling of resources and energies. Think about the outputs and inputs of elements of your design and be creative. An output that isn't cycled back into the system is pollution. An input that hasn't come from somewhere else in your system is resource intensive. A good example is battery chickens vs 'permaculture' chickens. Battery chickens need the expensive input of food and produced the output of poo which has to be got rid of. A permaculture chicken eats pests and food grown for it in the garden. It's 'outputs' go back into the soil to fertilise it. It is a truly multi-functional part of the permaculture system and it doesn't even know it!

Use edge effect. The places where two systems meet are rich and diverse places because they contain the inputs from both systems. In ecology, this is called the 'ecotone'. Places like wetlands, where rivers meet land, are naturally thronged with both aquatic and land-based life. Edges can be created in your designs by including lots of different elements like ponds, meadow and orchard.

Use three dimensional space. During your walk in the woods, take a look around you. Are things growing solely at knee height? This is something that human beings have the habit of doing. In nature, all of the possible space is used in three dimensions. Make use of vertical and horizontal space for example; include trees and plants of different heights and climbers and vines as well.

Use or mimic natural succession. A piece of bare earth will go through various stages for example, sparse vegetation and scrub before it finally reaches mature forest which is its most stable state. The above example of maximising three dimensional space works so well because it produces many yields whilst requiring little in the way of input. When you're thinking about growing;

consider how to use your time as well as space. How is what you are doing now, preparing the way for what comes next?

A note on permaculture design.
Permaculture is primarily a design process and can be used whether you are setting up a smallholding, building a house or starting a company. There are several stages to the process which can be remembered with the handy acronym SADIM. SADIM was discussed by Hedvig Murray back in section three. To remind you; SADIM stands for:

1. survey - This is your observation stage.
2. Analyse - What do you need from the design? What does the site or project need? What resources do you have? What limiting factors?
3. Design - Put your ideas down on paper.
4. Implement - Put those ideas into practice.
5. Maintain - Keep it going!

With thanks to:

Dr Dan Danahar: Dr Dan Danahar is married with two children. He is Biodiversity Coordinator at Dorothy Stringer High School, Biodiversity Officer for the Sussex Branch of Butterfly Conservation and Coordinator for Brighton & Hove's 'Big Nature'. His primary interest is bio-literacy, especially in a biodiversity context. Examples of his work can be viewed at: www.BigBiodiversityCount.org.uk

Beth Tilston: Beth Tilston is a positive change activist and writer from Brighton. She holds a Permaculture design certificate from Brighton Permaculture Trust. Beth tries to apply Permaculture ethics and principles across her life but most particularly at her allotment where she grows and keeps bees. Beth runs courses on natural beekeeping, is writing a book called Localise: A Toolkit for the Here and Now and works at a market garden.

Further resources.

If you want to find out more about Permaculture, Permaculture in a Nutshell by Patrick Whitefield is a great place to start. Whitefield is one of the leading lights in British permaculture and has written lots of books on the subject, most of which are published by Permanent Publications (www.permanent-publications.co.uk). Permanent Publications also publish books on subjects such as growing, natural building and self-sufficiency as well as producing the quarterly Permaculture Magazine (www.permaculture.co.uk).

To learn more, a permaculture introduction course would be a great place to start. These are usually weekend courses and can be found by through an internet search. Brighton Permaculture Trust (www.brightonpermaculture.org.uk) regularly run them. For a more in-depth insight into permaculture a two week 'Permaculture Design Course' is an option. Sometimes these are run over a number of weekends rather than an intensive two weeks. Building Sustainable Communities, the design course run by Brighton Permaculture Trust runs in this way.

Finally, Transition Initiatives are a great example of permaculture on a community scale. They were started in Totnes by Rob Hopkins who was a permaculture teacher. The local transition initiative is Transition Brighton and Hove (www.transition-brightonandhove.org.uk).

A genuinely practical and useful guide to doing things greener by Sarah Lewis-Hammond

The planet is littered not only with the oft pointless trophies of human profligacy but also with lists of going green top tips. While the former is the source of the latter, the latter is, more often than not, just as unhelpful as the former.

We all know these basic pillars of greening. What we need now is the money and motivation to do it.

Motivation.

This is sometimes hard to come by in any part of life. It's easy to find reasons for not doing things: work is busy, the kids keep painting the walls with custard, the towering stacks of washing up are the only things stopping the cracked plaster on the kitchen ceiling from becoming one with the kitchen floor.

But no matter how long you manage to avoid doing all that stuff on the list, one thing will remain true: the list is still there. It's not going away. The answer? Just get on with it.

If that feels all a little bit overwhelming, then do one thing at a time. There's only a handful of stuff anyway - food, water, energy, waste, transport. Spend a day or two every couple of months focussing on each topic and you'll be fully greened within the year.

Money.

Money, or lack thereof, is perhaps the only genuine reason for not cracking on with all those things we should all be doing. Insulating foam is expensive, recycled loo roll isn't as cheap as the value pack, and have you seen the price of a jar of pickles at the farmers' markets?

There is a secret to this though. Do one thing at a time and prioritise the money savers first.

Start with food. Brighton and Hove Food Partnership say changing the way you eat is the single biggest thing you can do to affect your ecological footprint, and Love Food Hate Waste say that with a little bit of care you can save up to fifty pounds a month on your food bills. So see what lovefoodhatewaste.com have to say about food planning and freezing and chewing down on left overs, and put the money you save away in a bank account.

In six months, you'll have saved 300 pounds, just the amount the Energy Savings Trust reckons it costs to insulate your loft, or draught exclude your house, which in turn can save you a couple of hundred pounds a year in energy bills. Sometimes there are even grants available to help pay for the cost of your insulation (subject to eligibility and availability) through Brighton and Hove Council's Warm Front Home Insulation programme (call the home energy efficiency officer on 01273 293144).

In fact, quite a lot of the stuff on that list is about saving money - from walking places instead of driving, to having a water metre installed, to switching your TV off standby. So maybe once you've done all that, you might just have saved enough for that jar of pickles after all.

Illustrators

Richard Ellis is an artist and filmmaker living and working in Sussex. Having studied in Media Arts and Animation, Richard has worked in a broad range of creative industries including post production and computer games, illustration for books and websites as well as teaching different aspects of digital media. He is currently working as a freelance illustrator. For more information visit: www.RichardEllisFilms.co.uk or email: mail@RichardEllisFilms.co.uk

Dean Hannon
20 Chorley Avenue
Brighton
BN2 8AQ
07865180475

Lucy Irving is an experienced freelance illustrator based in central Brighton, creating ideas-based, original and engaging imagery for both print and web media. Lucy's illustrations have been used in magazines, books, blogs, storyboards, online games, posters and flyers. Have a look at Lucy's work at www.irvingillustration.com, or contact her by email : lucy@irvingillustration.com

214

Rebecca Nunn

Becki embarked upon the delicate route of freelance illustration whilst standing in a tattoo parlour observing numerous clientèle choose the same generic designs  over and over again. This prompted her to begin personalising and tailoring images to suit each individual customer's body and wishes. Becki prides herself on having a knack for mimicking a variety of styles and for seamlessly incorporating these together in her art. Although she still loves creating unique tattoo designs, Becki now also does portraits, murals, band designs and other enticing assignments. Please feel free to discuss these at rexi.ink@hotmail.co.uk or e-mail her for upcoming exhibitions and other samples of work!

Chloë Louise Turner, born in Brighton, specialised in illustration on an Art Foundation before moving to Manchester to study History of Art and Design with Fine Art practice. She now lives in London but spends much of her time in Brighton. Some of Chloë Louise's most recent jobs have included working with the props dept. for Harry Potter, The Affordable Art Fair (running drawing workshops), and professional face painting in London Zoo. She works as a freelance artist and is keen to get involved with any creative venture, but particularly those in the interest of environmental consciousness, a subject about which she cares strongly. Her contact email is: chloe_turner85@hotmail.com

Louise Turner is an Arts graduate and qualified teacher has lived and worked in Brighton for over thirty years. Louise is a freelance artist who sells cards and stationary in local fairtrade shops and also works to commission. To contact her and for examples of her work please email: louise.turner@talk21.com

Leigh Wienburg is an artist of South African origin living happily in Brighton...Visit her website and say hi! www.leelu.net

Further thanks to:
The Natural Store: http://www.thenaturalstore.co.uk/
Eco Logic Cool: http://www.ecologiccool.com
City Car Club: http://www.citycarclub.co.uk/
The Eco Garage: http://www.theecogarage.co.uk/
Eco Btq: http://www.ecobtq.com/
Pulse Organics: http://www.pulseorganics.com/
Retail Therapy: http://www.retailtherapy.uk.com/

Contributors

David Ackroyd, Ann Baldridge, Lucie Britsch, Chris Callard, Daniel Campbell, Tom Chute, Aimee Cleary, Ellie Cooley, Jess Crocker, Dr Dan Danahar, Alice Doyle, Tom Druitt, Nick and Anna Eastwood, Karan Gardham, Sarah Lewis-Hammond, Marian Harding, Nick Harris, Amanda Hodgson, Philip Hunton, Hilary Knight, Joe Markendale, Sophie Adler Mckean, Hedvig Murray, Keith Nelson, Katie Ramsay, Sam Rose, Tanya Sadourian, Chris Seigal, Natalie Skinner, Suzan St Maur, Beth Tilston, David Treadwell, Sarah Walters,

Big Biodiversity Count, City Car Club, Court Lodge Organics, Four Seasons Fuel, Get Growing, Green Man and Van, Green Up Your Act Education, Greenminded, Growing Up Green Nursery, Grow Your Neighbours Own, Harvest Brighton and Hove, Infinity Foods, Mid Sussex Wood Recyling Project, Nigel's Eco Store, St Martin's Tea Rooms, Sussex Enterprise, South Downs Joint Committee, The Big Lemon Bus Company, The Original Hut Company,

Proof Readers: Lucie Britsch, Nicky Carter, Danica Lesser, Sandra Pegram, Don Ramsay, Annika Thornton, Beth Williams and Ellie Wilson.